MUSIC IS IN OUR
BLOOD

JIM NEGLIA

InfusedMedia Co. LLC
www.infusedmedia.co
1-888-251-6088

"Ancestral spirits of your father's house [do] not identify
you by looks or stature but by the DNA they buried deep
down [within] your blood." –Ikechukwu Izuakor

After a nearly forty-year hiatus, my father and I sat down together
and shared a meal. Our conversation covered many areas, but focused
on his immigration from Italy to the United States, our heritage, and
our ancestors. For the first time in decades, I heard family stories I never
knew. I learned about my great aunts and uncles, their parents, and how
generations of Neglias were devoted to music. We reminisced about his
sister, my aunt Maria, who would give me and my brother violin lessons
when we were very young. During our meal, I learned more about my
father's side of the family than I had known my entire lifetime.

It was after this meeting that I first contemplated writing a book
on my ancestry. Now, armed with more knowledge than ever before, I
felt I had enough to connect the dots between the Neglias of the past
to those of the present. In this book, I hope to illustrate our deepest
family bond, music.

And so, I began.

I researched, identified, and recreated our family tree, focusing on
my father's side. I traced our tree back to my great-great-grandfather in
Sicily in the early part of the 19th century.

Devotion to music has been constant, as most in our family are
musicians. And at least two of my ancestors had not only a deep love
of music but demonstrated their talents through illustrious careers. My
grandfather's brother, my great uncle, Francesco Paolo (22 May 1874
† 31 July 1932), is one of them. He was a prolific composer, concert
violinist, conductor, and educator. Struggling to find work in Italy prior
to World War I, Francesco relocated to Hamburg, Germany, where he
flourished and gained the respect of the community and beyond. His
popularity had grown so much that he opened the Neglia Conservatory

in Hamburg and later another school in Legnano, Italy. He was friends, colleagues, and collaborators with such personalities as Enrico Caruso, Felix Weingartner, Richard Strauss, Marco Enrico Bossi, and Giacomo Puccini, to name a few. He led a fascinating career which I will cover in-depth in this book.

The other family member that reached worldwide acclaim is my father's sister, my aunt Maria (7 August 1927 † 27 August 2016). She was a gifted violinist and child prodigy. During the 1950s and 1960s, Maria was a regular guest on the Ed Sullivan Show (appearing 24 times), as well as the Johnny Carson, Mike Douglas, and Joey Bishop shows, and most importantly, on the Arthur Godfrey Show. It was on her first television broadcast with Godfrey that she was discovered.

Florida's Senator George Smathers, along with fellow-show business stars Bob Hope, Arthur Godfrey, Jackie Gleason, Martha Raye, Kate Smith, Jack Paar, and Ed Sullivan, wrote to the U. S. senate to attest to Maria's talents and extraordinary personality. Ultimately through a special vote, Smathers helped clear the path for her United States citizenship. This special legislation was approved and signed by President Dwight Eisenhower, who quickly became friends with my aunt Maria. Maria performed at the White House several times, for President Eisenhower but also for President Nixon.

Francesco and Maria's silent influence showered over me from the day I was born into the family. There are others in our extended family with musical talent, but I feel these two stand out from the others. I hope to illustrate the many parallels between my past ancestors with the present family, including myself.

I spent a lot of time debating if we inherit music or any craft from past generations or if we learn via exposure. I understood the discrepancies between the two and began my research. My goal wasn't to qualify what I believed but to understand better genetics and how they impact the family tree.

DNA or deoxyribonucleic acid is the self-replicating material present in nearly all living organisms and is the main constituent of chromosomes.

When using an autosomal test (a term used in genetic genealogy to describe DNA inherited from the autosomal chromosomes) like the one they use in Ancestry˚ or My Heritage™, the results can go back up to eight generations. Knowing and understanding this timeline, I chose to trace our family tree back 200 years, starting with Domenico Neglia.

Researcher Miriam Mosey, a neuroscientist at the Karolinska Institute in Sweden, said: "The idea that an externally imposed (music) practice regime can and will lead to expertise seems to be wrong. Rather, an innate ability should also not be seen in a deterministic way. Naturally, practice will almost always lead to an increase in ability, but not necessarily to high-level expertise." The study concluded that genetics play a prominent role in musical abilities, much more than practicing, regardless of the hours put in.

Drawing on my musical abilities and those of my ancestors, my belief aligns with the concept that our musical talents are passed down from our ancestors. Those who have others in the household who can nourish a budding musician will help to increase or heighten those inherited talents, but I believe that music is in our bloodline.

My roots are deeply embedded in European traditions. My father's family hails from the small town of Enna, Sicily, and my mother and her family were from Corleone, also in Sicily. My siblings and I are first-generation Italian-Americans. We are all musicians, all making our living in our field. My children and those of my siblings are either musicians or musically inclined.

In 1986 I made the journey to Enna for the first time, and while reflecting on that visit, emotional memories came flooding back. Most prominent were my footsteps walking through my great uncle's theater located in Enna's Town Hall, which houses Francesco's piano, much of his furniture, musical scores, his conducting baton, two violins, and other personal belongings.

F.P. Neglia's Piano (above) and violin (below),
on display in Town Hall, Enna, Sicily

F.P. Neglia's metronome and baton

While researching our family, I obtained a great deal of information on both Francesco and Maria. I was happy to find articles, letters, concert reviews, and other documents. Much of the material I discovered on Francesco, especially from his Hamburg days, was in either Italian or German. To better understand Francesco, I began the painstaking task of translating each letter, article, and review into English. This process took me a good deal of time, but ultimately, I accomplished my goal. I was proud to gain the much-needed knowledge and understanding to begin sharing his story. Not only did I find the act of translating the precious articles interesting, but I also gained a deeper understanding of my family's devotion to music.

Apart from the musical bonds passed down through generations, I learned of another unexpected similarity. My great uncle's son, Giuseppe, affectionately known as Peppino, kept a journal on his family and life's progression. I used many journal entries in my first two books to highlight my journey through music and life itself. It might simply be coincidental, but understanding just how deep our roots are connected, I feel that the act of documenting is also a shared art between the generations.

Jim 1964 – one year old

I am proud of my heritage and bloodline and hope to illustrate our deep connections to music and each other in this book.

REFLECTIONS

"Children begin by loving their parents; after time they judge them; rarely, if ever, do they forgive them." –Oscar Wilde

Like many marriages, my parents' ended in a divorce. The circumstances which led them to its dissolution began in the earliest days of my memory. As a result of the split, I became somewhat estranged from my father. For roughly 35 years, we rarely spoke, communicating via email, with an occasional phone call.

Growing up fatherless, yet needing guidance beyond my mother's strength, I turned to my oldest brother, Joe. Although I needed him, during my teenage years, in my young, immature mindset, I resisted his help.

I struggled with the hierarchy of the family; I couldn't figure it out. My emotional journey through adolescence only helped impede the goodwill of my brother. Thinking back all these years, I could have survived a much easier teen passage with less resistance and more understanding if I had just listened to my inner self and not the demons whispering in my ear.

As the period of uncertainty passed, and with the encouragement and support of my brother, our relationship matured.

To this day, Joe is my go-to person from whom I draw advice, counsel, and reassurance. Although I believe I know what I am going to do, and my wife and I discuss everything imaginable, I still will call Joe for security, if not affirmation. Much to his credit, he knows how to react to my questions and statements, never discounting them. On the contrary, he will mostly find other options to offer, other ideas that might lead to the same conclusion, but without some of the baggage that might be looming. I find his ability to balance these aspects to be a rare trait in a person, and I am happy to have him as my brother.

My oldest brother, Joe, and me –December 2007

A great deal of time passed since I had any contact with my father when, one day, out of the blue, my phone rang.

My father, who was now 80 years old, called to request we get together; at his age, I imagined he was looking to cleanse himself of decades of neglect. Perhaps his life was coming to an end, and he wanted to ask for forgiveness? I had no idea what his real motivation was, nor did it ultimately matter. In nearly no time I decide to share with my father where we live and invite him for dinner a few days later.

Our sons knew of their grandfather and much of what had transpired with our relationship. Opening our hearts and allowing someone to share their needs was important enough to open our home and share the table. I felt this was the right message to share with our sons, and hopefully, they would gain some perspective on the events that would later help them in life.

I called my siblings and explained our father's phone call. I shared why I thought it was important to see him and why we should show our children, nieces, and nephews what grown-ups do in cases like this.

My siblings agreed to come with their children whom our father never knew or met. We set a date and time.

I hoped that the gathering could help me achieve resolution with a 40-year-old relationship that had faded decades earlier.

When our father arrived at my house, he was unrecognizable to me. I saw a different person than I had known in my early, impressionable years. I had him fixed in my memory as a young, muscular man who could lift a house on command. When I was nine years old, I stepped on a rusty nail that went through my foot. His immediate reaction was to sit me down and suck the rust from my open wound. That was then, and this is now; how time changes all. I no longer had any unanswered questions. Every feeling, doubt, question, and curiosity vanished as he walked up the path to our home.

A year or so after our dinner gathering, I first conceptualized writing a book on our family heritage. Apart from my older siblings, no one else could give me the information I needed to begin, except my father. Much like needing to know a parent's medical history, I felt compelled to learn as much about our family's heritage as I could. Now, at peace with my past, I was able to work unencumbered.

Three generations
(*left to right*) My father Joseph, my brother Joe,
and Grandfather Angelo Neglia —1956

I wrote to my father and asked some basic questions about our heritage; I received a response, which read in part:

September 3, 2013

My cousin Giuseppe Neglia, son of Francesco Paolo, wrote to my dad years ago when his daughter, known as "La Pucci" (Maria), married.

Francesco's second wife's name was Teresa, and my Mother (Dora Biondi) lived with her while waiting to get a permit to join us in the United States, which happened in 1955.

Giuseppe (Peppino) bought a magnificent store of imported leather gloves for Teresa to enjoy a comfortable livelihood in wealthy San Remo.

There was a younger son of Teresa and Francesco named Franco Neglia, who wrote a book of poetry dedicated to his Father, copyrighted in 1951 by Editore Gheroni in Torino, printed in Italy.

The dedication is: A Mio Padre, al suo dolore, alla sua Gloria, alla sua morte, ora e sempre (To my Father, to his pain, to his glory, to his death, now and forever.) Dedicated in Sanremo in the Summer of 1951. A copy of this book of poetry entitled *Canto agli uomini d'oggi* (I sing to the men of today) is in my office next to your book *Onward and Upward*.

He continues: "My days are getting shorter; that's called the circle of life, and I wish to clear some totally wrong sentiments that just went astray.

Ti penso sempre con sincere affetto (I always think of you with heartfelt affection)."

I suspected I knew what wrong sentiments he referred to and believed that he needed to take care of business now if there was something to clear up.

A few weeks later, I received this unexpected email.

20 September 2013

There is no purpose in writing my "memoirs," except that I have often wished to share my personal feelings with people I genuinely love. It is no fun to remember moments in my life that I hope no one in my family will have to experience.

No, I have no intention to publish it; however, you are free to if you desire, nothing I write is new; all these experiences have been part of many other lives, yet these are my thoughts and ideas I have had to deal with, my driving thought is 'the same hammer that breaks the glass also forges the steel.'

It was clear his time was limited, and he spent the past week, if not months, reflecting on his own life. If he genuinely believes in a just and merciful God, he knew he would have to answer to a higher power.

I arrived in the United States on 18 October 1948. The anticipation of prosperity, work, and success with a positive attitude was present, but dealing with the painful past was unexpected. I had first to identify how deep and painful it all had been up to that point.

In my birth city of Trieste (in 1929), my Father, who stayed clear of the Mussolini regime, had moved to the farthest Italian city. [He] worked nights in a movie theater synchronizing music to a featured First World War movie scene captured by an Italian General before sound was available. Things were not moving successfully for his business even as he had several violin students to help with the stipend. In 1930, my sister Maria always imitated the students and mimicked them with a toy violin, called my dad's attention by playing a perfectly in tune scale, much to everyone's amazement. As a result, my dad would include my sister as a serious student before the age of three.

Maria Neglia – age 3

Little did he know she would surpass everyone's ability, agility, and memory.

In the meantime, with the new popularity of radio, lessons diminished gradually, and hunger was at our back door. My dad and sister worked out a few selections and found a convenient street where they would perform for hours while at three years old, I handled the plate for the gifts, and my mom kept me warm.

When Maria was nearly five years old, the Theater owner where my father worked asked to hear her play, out of politeness, remained amazed at her ability and suggested having her perform once in his theater. My father rejected the offer as, at that time, children were not allowed to perform, except for gypsies.

Shortly, one performance was agreed, no stipend, just niceties.

That performance was a spectacle, and the audience was ecstatic and demanded more and more. A deal was quickly arranged, and other theaters in several large cities heard about the child prodigy and wanted to offer her to their audiences. Soon Germany's most popular performing venues knocked on our door requesting the same. This was followed by years of contracts throughout Germany. In August 1938, Maria performed at the renowned Winter Garden Theater in Berlin, Germany.

In 1936, I was placed in a boarding school for my education. My parents were moving to a different city every month due to my sister Maria's success. My first elementary grade was successful but confusing due to the constant moving and due to the fact we had no domicile to call home.

I learned to make friends quickly and got used to losing them faster. By age seven, it was firmly established the favorable location would be Firenze, where my uncle Aldo Biondi, a representative for Fernet-Branca, was married to Margherita and had a daughter named Olga, a bright girl somewhat older than I.

Maria performing at the Winter Garden Theater,
Berlin, Germany, 1938 – age 10

As Uncle Aldo had a problematic marriage relationship,
I was not supposed to live with them but have them
pay me visits from time to time. A safe place to live
and attend school was in a convent with nuns; after
visiting them, I voiced my unexpected opinion that I
would undoubtedly escape from that lifestyle at the first
occasion. My plea was accepted and believed as a serious
warning; it seems my parents believed me.

The decision was then changed to Bologna, where
Teresina Nanni, a good friend of my father, lived with
a nephew she had adopted and raised past graduating
from the University. He was now married to Agnese,

who delivered him three boys, Roberto, Francesco (my age), and Giorgio, just a few years apart in age.

Teresina had been a successful dress and hat designer and maker in her youth and had never married, a very warm and genuinely affectionate lady about 4 foot 9 inches tall with a somewhat contorted face, a humped shoulder, and a very protruding chin.

She would visit me at the Collegio weekly, a sight of hope and caring though I had to put up with the boys ridiculing me about her appearance.

This email represents the last time we had any contact. Ten months later, I learned my father passed, on 12 May 2014, when my half-sister called with the news.

With my father in 2013 at our visit.

MAURIZIO AGRÒ

"Eventually, everything connects—people, ideas, objects. The
quality of the connections is the key to quality per se."
—Charles Eames

Portrait of Francesco Paolo Neglia by Arturo Zanieri (1870-1955)

At the same time I was working on my family tree, I began to
outline other chapters in this book. I was formulating ideas, thinking
about how I can join my heritage with some current events. While doing
so, I quickly found that writing about current events was much easier
than researching my family tree.

I had, in my possession, several books written about my great uncle.
I had already been in the process of translating them from Italian so I

could learn more about his life and career. During this time, I decided to reach out to the author of one book, Maurizio Agrò. Maurizio is a direct descendant of Liborio Neglia, brother of Francesco Paolo.

Maurizio was able to fill in many of the much-needed missing pieces of our family tree. I learned a great deal while translating his book, as well as through our email correspondences. Maurizio shared that he received much information from Maria Evelina Neglia, his mother's aunt. Maria Evelina had been on good terms with her cousin Peppino, son of Francesco Paolo.

Although Mario Barbieri wrote the first biography on Francesco Paolo, titled *Life, Art, and Thoughts of an Italian Musician, with a foreword by Renzo Bossi*, it lacks details and explanations of Neglia's compositions. Maurizio's book, *Nella vita e nell'arte, La prima biografia ufficiale* (*In Life and in Art, The First Official Biography*) covers both Francesco's life and many of his compositions. Maurizio shares a rare in-depth analysis of my great uncle's music.

Maurizio shared with me many letters between Francesco and his son Peppino. In addition to the personal letters, we found other information through the personal journal entries of Peppino himself. Many of the chapters about Francesco Paolo in this book are borrowed loosely from Maurizio's book on our great uncle.

Peppino and I never spoke, nor did we know each other; however, it seems we shared not only our DNA and music genes but the desire to keep a journal as well; I was fascinated.

It was Peppino who shared his father's library of musical repertoire. Peppino began to maintain relationships with the musicians, musicologists, composers, and critics of the time. There was Giulio Confalonieri, Luigi Perrachio, Renzo Bossi, Mario Barbieri, Massimo Mila, Sergio Martinotti, Jacopo Napoli, Alfredo Mandelli, and conductors Ottavio Ziino and Umberto Berrettoni, to name a few. Our art, once again, takes center stage, binding our ancestral background.

Giuseppe (Peppino) Neglia, the son of Francesco Paolo – 1970

Peppino took up his late father's cause. From 1939 until Peppino's death in 1974, he arranged many performances of his father's music. Peppino also found a path to publish Francesco's music. His music was printed and distributed by two small publishing houses in Italy: Edizioni Musica di Genova and Augusta Edizioni di Torino.

In August 1921, during Francesco's summer holidays, he returned to Hamburg. He went to reconnect with the German musical world he left behind. He succeeded in obtaining from the Hamburg Municipal Theater's Superintendence an offer to present his only opera, *Zelia,* the following winter season.

Unfortunately, he did not have enough finances to stay in Hamburg and returned to Vanzago to resume teaching classes. Ultimately, the performance of *Zelia* did not take place due to both political and economic reasons. Neglia then tried to have a performance of *Zelia* in Milan; however, he sadly documented; "Amid adversity and hardship, I found time and a way to write an opera in three acts. But for the same economic reason, I will have to close it hermetically to oblivion because a torturer of an impresario, to have my opera presented at the Teatro Dal Verme in Milan, demands a sum that I do not have."

In July 1974, fifty-three years later, and just three months before Peppino's death, Peppino fully funded a performance of *Zelia*. Peppino met his goal, and we can only imagine the joy on the face of Francesco from above.

ZELIA Billboard - performance on Sunday, 7 July 1974,
in the city of Enna, at the Theater of Lombardy Castle

Maria Evelina took up where Peppino left off, pursuing all possible performances of Francesco's works available to her. Maria Evelina stayed with this crusade until Maurizio took over in 1999. Maurizio managed to get in touch with Francesco's niece, Giuseppina, daughter of Peppino.

A few years after Maurizio took up the family quest, he discovered magnetic tapes where Francesco's music was performed live and captured for all future generations to hear. For the most part, these recordings are all on YouTube for all who wish to enjoy them.

I made a great deal of progress. For the first time since contemplating sharing my findings, I felt I was on my way.

A scene from the opera *Zelia* –July 1974

THE NEGLIA FAMILY

I have included our family tree in Appendix I at the end of this book. The family tree that I am sharing here, is an abridged version which highlights the members discussed in greater detail in this book.

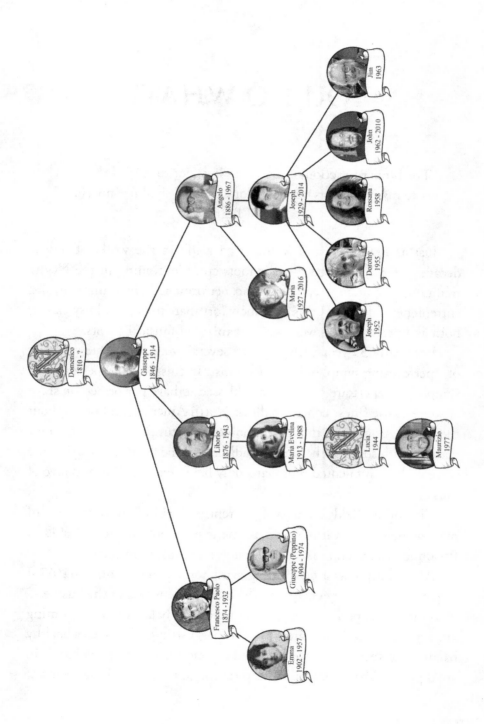

YOU DO WHAT?

"The proper function of man is to live, not to exist. I shall not
waste my days in trying to prolong them. I shall use my time."
                    –Neil Peart

Just as Francesco and Maria lived a life in the world of music,
decades later, I followed in their footsteps. Continuing in the Neglia
tradition, a tradition steeped in music, performance, entertainment, and
entrepreneurial skills, I was extremely fortunate to enjoy a busy career,
both as a performer, as well as an organizer of musical events.

For nearly 35 years, I have worn several work hats. One was that
of a performing symphonic percussionist. In this, I would perform the
symphonic repertoire weekly. I was blessed to have performed on stage
at some of the finest concert halls in North America, and throughout
the world. Along with those symphonic opportunities, I performed for
decades with some of the finest headliners in the business. Sharing the
stage with such talented musicians only heightened my joy and love of
music.

The other field I am still currently working in is as part of
management. My various management positions include Orchestra
Personnel Manager, music coordinator, and music contractor.

After retiring as a performing symphonic percussionist in 2017, I
began to focus all my energy on the management side of the business.

During my performing career, I needed to balance my performing
and management duties carefully. At times, I struggled to keep a healthy
balance between the two as I needed to practice and keep my hands in
good playing shape, as well as keep thorough notes on all the events of

the day while at work in my management capacity. At times, both of these were very time-consuming.

As a manager, I hope to provide a professional, stress-free working environment so all can perform at their highest ability. Although that might sound like an easy task, at times it feels like there are forces doing everything to prevent me from reaching my goal.

Johnny Mathis –30 April 2010
The first of dozens of performances together

Each day when I arrive at work, my approach is identical, whether it is at my symphony job (currently at the Jacksonville Symphony) or a freelance event as a music contractor. I enter at the appointed time and proper location with a smile on my face and a bounce in my step. You would be surprised how infectious this approach can be; I believe that positive energy is transferable and enters others through their subconscious.

Conversely, on the off chance that I am having a slightly off day, it is instantly felt by most, if not all. I do my best to avoid those negative feelings, but I am human and suffer just like the rest. The one unfortunate side of what I do is that a person in my position does not have the option of having a *bad day*, ever.

Weird Al was performing on his accordion.
I took these photos from my vantage point on stage left. —2018

The various hats I wear, that of an orchestra personnel manager, music contractor, and music coordinator, share similar responsibilities; however, they have varying aspects. Music contracting and music coordinating are mostly interchangeable terms. A contractor is more of an on-hand position where I attend the rehearsals and performances, however, where a music coordinator oversees the full production on a tour that is traveling from city to city.

An orchestra personnel manager's first duties are to uphold the articles spelled out in their CBA (collective bargaining agreement). This CBA is a document that the membership and management negotiate. Although the negotiations can sometimes feel contentious, both parties give and take on many details and live with the results until the next negotiation. The CBA is a set of rules ratified by the players, union, and management, which govern the particular organization.

As a music contractor and coordinator, I need to understand the CBA language of the various cities where I will be booking performances.

Each city will have its own rules, pay scale, and set of guidelines that I need to learn, understand, and ultimately implement.

with Brian Stokes Mitchell –December 2011

In all cases, specific skills are measurably more critical than others, and it takes time for the required skills to develop and take hold. In my field, one needs effective, efficient written and oral communication skills; knowledge and experience with electronic media and their associated American Federation of Musician agreements; superior organizational skills and the ability to prioritize responsibilities to maximize efficiency and institutional goals; and the ability to work under pressure with a wide variety of personalities while exhibiting patience, understanding, and a sense of humor. Additionally, the knowledge of symphonic repertoire is highly beneficial as is familiarity with orchestra industry practices and traditions.

RAP Artist Nelly, along with me, Charlie Descarfino
and Jimmy Musto —September 2016

Beyond those skills, particular administrative habits make my life easier in my work as an orchestra personnel manager. I need to create and maintain a musician contact and hiring list and manage payroll. I need to keep the operation staff up to date with hired personnel. I must track all services (rehearsals and performances), musicians' paid and unpaid leave requests, maternity and paternity leave, family, and medical leave while keeping the local union informed of any contractual issues. I attend all rehearsals and performances where the orchestra is employed. For those I cannot attend, I designate the assistant personnel manager to take my place.

In my full-time orchestra position with the symphony, I answer to the General Manager, the CEO, and the Music Director. I need to arrange tenure-track and probationary musician's meetings. I must carefully balance out the needs of the musicians while keeping in mind the needs and expectations of the association; this is no easy task, I assure you. I need to keep the ship running smoothly and straight.

The icing on my work cake is that after each issue, complaint, problem, or request, I must document the episode in writing. Contemporaneous notes are paramount, as, at times, I might need to refer to something that took place a week, month, or year ago. All I have are my notes to bring the entire episode back into focus. I call this part of my duties the *icing* because while documenting, I consider if the issue at hand might be good to include in an upcoming publication. I do my best to take notes that are thorough and mark the day with stark factual details. All of my notes begin with the date, day, time, and usually the weather report. Today is Monday, 31 May 2021; the temperature is a warm 81, with the winds coming from the NNW. Sharing these details only lends to the credibility of what is to come.

With the conductor, Jerry Steichen, and Neil Sedaka
in Woodstock, New York –July 2011

During my career, I realized that most of what I do in my professional life has to do with organizing all the details that makes the organization run smoothly and to oversee the execution of those details. It is imperative for me to think about every possible aspect of each event. Each rehearsal or performance carries a unique footprint of needs and requirements; the circumstances of each unfold as each takes place.

When working on each gig, I am acutely aware that some disaster could just be waiting to happen. My job is to ensure that there are no disasters. It is my responsibility to lay out each project and dissect it from start to finish. When looking at each event, I carefully think about what may happen. I must head off whatever pitfalls might occur to prevent a fiasco.

As the years have progressed, it has become easier for me to ward off potential problems. Experience is something that only comes with time, age, and countless mishaps along the way. I have taken all the past experiences, good and bad, and learned from them. After all these years, dealing with these issues has become second nature to me.

The Ambassador of the Great American Songbook,
Michael Feinstein –March 2017

I have been in the position where we were just 40 minutes away from the start of a rehearsal, and a trumpet player called to say they would be late. I'm not talking five minutes late, but an hour. Resolving issues like this is a multi-tiered process, starting with high-volume phone calls, followed by complete disclosure of the problem to the music director or visiting conductor.

In actual emergency cases such as this, I go to my trusty iPhone and hit "trumpet." Within seconds, every trumpet player in my database pops up. Not only did I program my iPhone to show me the musician's phone number, but also their geographic location. The player with the closest address to the site of the service receives the first call.

Over the years, I have learned it is my complete responsibility to keep order on the stage. I am responsible for virtually everything that happens during an orchestra rehearsal or performance. It is a massive responsibility.

Ky-Mani Marley (son of Bob Marley) at The United
Nations Headquarters, New York –July 2015

Over the course of decades, I have learned a solid life lesson: managing is an art. Like any great work, it becomes more valuable over time.

Composer Karel Husa, Harrisburg, Pennsylvania
–November 1989

Composer Tan Dun at the New Jersey Performing Arts Center
Newark, New Jersey –January 2016

With Game of Thrones Assistant conductor Michael
Sobie, and composer and conductor Ramin Djawadi,
Jones Beach, New York —September 2019

While much of my work life includes a great deal of business, what I call clutter, my personal life has moved in the complete opposite direction. After sharing my thoughts on being a manager, I feel it is important to share the other side of my thinking. The reduction of clutter from my personal space has influenced my overall approach to life and ultimate happiness. My philosophy of less is more peaked back in 2017 after reading *the life-changing magic of tidying up: the Japanese art of decluttering and organizing* by Marie Kondo. After reading this tiny, magical book, I went on a purging spree. I have removed all unnecessary things from our home, my home office, and my work office and feel nothing but peace as a result. In doing so, I have embraced the newness of my life, which allows me to better deal with the complexities of my work life. Although it felt seemingly perfect before, my home life has only improved by accepting the concept of less is more.

Composer Marvin Laird and Cubby O'Brien at the New Jersey Performing Arts Center, Newark, New Jersey. "Cubby" is an American drummer and former child actor, best known as one of the original Mouseketeers on the weekday ABC television program *The Mickey Mouse Club* –April 2012

I have never believed that all "things" are necessary—I mean, how many things can I have? Where am I going to put all my things? Where did I misplace my things? As a direct result of my busy, cluttered work life and fascination with downsizing, I developed a minimalistic view on life, which sparked my yearning for serenity when not working.

My work life parallels that of a cyclone—I feel like the fictional character Pig-Pen from the famous Charles Schultz comic Peanuts, constantly surrounded by the cloud of details. It is not only my desire to create a complete juxtaposition between my work life and my now peaceful home life but a necessity.

As someone who travels quite a bit and has been doing it for many years, I have mastered the art of packing. When going on long trips, in the beginning, I would pack everything, including the kitchen sink. As time progressed, I would lay everything on my bed, and then cut my *needs* in half, and then cut that half in half, leaving me with a fraction of what I thought I needed. After jumping that hurdle and surviving it, I knew that process was transferable to my family. It just took many more years to work through.

In the process of downsizing, while looking through some tucked-away, overflowing boxes, I stumbled across a nostalgic find—all of my past agenda books. Each year is represented, from 1988 through 2019, all waiting for further inspection.

I couldn't help but think about my old friend and pen pal Ray Benjamin and his red journals. I remember the advice he offered me over three decades ago. "Jim, keep a written record of all those events you feel are worthy to note. I think you are going to have a very impressive career." I did just that. I followed Ray's advice and wrote and wrote over the years.

Within the pages of these agendas, there were many details that came alive during my purging session. I relived so many beautiful memories of my past work and I had the privilege of sharing many of those stories in my first two books, *Onward and Upward* and *Center Stage*.

Natalie Merchant, American alternative rock singer-songwriter
Count Basie Theatre, Red Bank, New Jersey –4 October 2013

After peering through the pages of my past date books, I had this thought: there is no mistaking why I feel I have put a lifetime of effort and dedication into my craft over the past 35 years. So many memories came pouring back. Memories of working with old friends and making new ones. I had noted when I brought a newly purchased instrument on a particular gig. The numerous commutes to gig after gig; the long, lonely hours in the car, munching on sunflower seeds to help me stay awake in the wee hours of the night during my seemingly endless drive home. All roads lead back to my commitment to the arts.

One route that I traveled the most, some 80 times per year in my memory, is from our New Jersey home to the home of the Harrisburg Symphony, located in Pennsylvania's capital. That commute took place for about eight years, and the drive was a grueling 180 miles each way.

On stage with The Harrisburg Symphony –November 1987

Years later, the reality of traveling from city to city switched to country to country. Powerful stories from my years of foreign trips, performances, and experiences came flooding back. These intense memories were brought to light while I thumbed through the pages of these precious datebooks.

Hours of combing through the books also yielded a list of the organizations which played a contributing role in assisting me in arriving at the life I enjoy today.

In *Center Stage*, referring to the year 2016, I wrote:

"Reflecting on the past 18 months of opportunities, I compiled a list of accomplishments I felt I could continue to grow. On my list are The Game of Thrones tour, Zelda, Symphony of the Goddesses, Final Fantasy, and Hans Zimmer Tours. Along with those tours, I worked with various organizations on the *Nike* experience, Michelin Tires festivities, and the New York Fashion show with Michael Kors. All of these productions fell well outside of the non-profit model and became part of my new focus."

On the Throne at Game of Thrones!

Michelin Tires production, Palm Springs, California –March 2017

Il Volo at the New Jersey Performing Arts Center,
Newark, New Jersey –October 2014

with Chuck Berry and his friend, in Morristown, at the
Mayo Center for the Performing Arts. –May 1997

Hans Zimmer, at Radio City Music Hall, NY
City just before the performance. –2017

Il Divo at the Wells Fargo Arena, Pennsylvania
access badge –30 August 2017

NIKE Orchestra set up at Moynihan Station, New York City
–March 2016

Michael Kors at the Spring Studio, New York City –2017

Tommy Tallarico, American video game music composer,
me, and conductor Emmanuel Fratianni
Video Games Live, in Jacksonville, Florida –20 February 2020

With conductor Jacques Lacombe and American saxophonist,
Branford Marsalis at the New Jersey Performing Arts
Center, Newark, New Jersey –September 2015

Apple and Apple TV. I secured the orchestra for the world premiere of "The Morning Show," which premiered at Josie Robertson Plaza and David Geffen Hall, Lincoln Center for the Performing Arts in New York –28 October 2019

Final Fantasy Performances, with composer Nobuo Uematsu for the 30th anniversary of Final Fantasy at Carnegie Hall New York, New York –2018

All-Access badge for Radio City Music Hall's *Back to
the Future* 30th anniversary performances –2015

with actor, Christopher Lloyd and film composer, Alan Silvestri
after the show at Radio City Music Hall, New York City
–17 October 2015

On the set of the movie, *Joe Gould's Secret* with Stanley Tucci, on location in Brooklyn, New York –April 1999

Concert Pianist, Lang Lang –October 2008

American actress and singer Bernadette Peters
–November 2016

Concert Pianist, André Watts (center) at the New
Jersey Performing Arts Center –2015

Actor and comedian Sandy Hackett —2014

Actress and singer Debbie Gravitte —June 2016

I feel the direction of my life has moved to areas that support my recent comfort with downsizing. Much like Francesco Paolo experiencing contentment through his love of family and music, our needs revert to the essentials: embracing music, having a place to live, food on our table, and love in our hearts and home.

In October 2017, shortly after leaving my job at the New Jersey Symphony, I was forced to dig deep into my contracting and music coordinating abilities. I needed to decide what I was going to do with the next chapter of my life.

Until this point, I cannot recall ever having a period in my life where I was bored, without goals, and not being laser-focused on the future. But then, I felt without daily purpose; I began to abandon all future ideas; I lost all interest. It was a dark and challenging time for me, one where, at times, I felt hopeless and lost. Although I thought I had diverse abilities and a few very valuable clients to draw on, I was floundering without the daily structure of the symphony.

Violinist Sarah Chang –2015

With Israeli-American violinist Pinchas Zukerman and friend
—22 January 2017

I had worked for a few high-profile organizations that secured me as their music coordinator on various North American and European projects. To pull myself back from jumping into the monstrous chasm standing before me, I knew it was time to get back in touch with those folks who had employed me in the past. It was time to pick myself up and address the negative cloud which was surrounding me.

All United States touring preparations were somewhat similar to orchestra contracting, as I needed to secure the members of the orchestra, prepare union contracts and payroll, and so forth. Preparing a short leg of a tour required a few more layers, like arranging for security, securing dressing rooms at the arena, preparing lists for the venue, travel logistics, catering instructions, as well as how to enter the building without getting lost! Often, upon entering a large arena, we are sent through a labyrinth of corridors before finding our dressing rooms. Even the placement of signage falls under my responsibilities on these tour dates.

I am constantly trying to develop creative ideas to save money for the producers: innovative yet legitimate. One way of saving cost is to see if there are opportunities to use the same musicians in multiple cities.

If two cities had a complementing performance schedule, within two or three days of the first performance, and the cities were within 150 miles of each other, I could use the same musicians. Why is this helpful? Because we were able to reduce the number of rehearsals needed for a multi-leg production, thus saving money.

Cellist Yo-Yo Ma –May 2013

Tony Curtis backstage for *Some Like It Hot* –1 October 2005

Larry Storch backstage for *Some Like It Hot*
−1 October 2005

With violinist Vadim Gluzman and my wife, Sasha
−September 2012

A typical "in and out" arena production in one city would have a 12–1 p.m. choir rehearsal, followed by a 2–5 p.m. rehearsal for the choir and orchestra, and usually an 8:00 p.m. performance that evening. If that performance took place in Portland, Oregon, and the next day we had a performance in Seattle–about a three and a half-hour drive–we could cancel the 12–1 p.m. choir rehearsal and change the three-hour rehearsal to a one-hour soundcheck in the new venue. These small changes could potentially save thousands of dollars each time.

Scottish percussionist Evelyn Glennie –2005

If I could use this model many times on a thirty-city tour, the company that hired me would realize substantial savings, thus making me their golden music coordinator. No matter what one may think, no matter how large or small a production, the end game was to make as much money for the producers as possible. There was no tenure in contracting, only passing on savings; that was the best job security out there!

Performing with Ringling Bros. and Barnum & Bailey
The Meadowlands Arena, East Rutherford, New Jersey –1988

Composer Peter Schickele—Mr. P.D.Q. Bach—
at the Morris Museum Theater, Morristown, New Jersey
–October 1995

The only downside for me was that once I won a bid and the tour was up and running, there was little left to do except wait for the actual performance dates to arrive. Once they concluded, I was able to send in my invoices. This kind of work was a far cry from the daily operations of a symphony orchestra, and I was missing that aspect of my former life.

The productions, some of which I would attend, were exhilarating, and for those days where I can physically play my role, the time passed quickly. But for the days where I was sending someone in my place, due to performance location, the time would pass slower than a snail crossing the road. The slow pace of my work led to the lack of my daily excitement and desire. Life back as an orchestra personnel manager was required.

Opera singer Frederica von Stade at the New Jersey Performing Arts Center, Newark, New Jersey –January 2010

Although my desire to work with a symphony orchestra was genuine, there was one huge obstacle standing before me. An orchestra has to announce an opening. Generally speaking, once a personnel manager accepts a job, they will remain there for their entire career. But before winning a position, I needed to wait for an announcement of an opening in an orchestra. This wasn't a snail crossing the road; this was more like watching the grass grow. In my eyes, winning a personnel position with a major orchestra would be equivalent to winning the pick-six lottery.

Feeling it would be a very long time before I'd have the opportunity to interview for a personnel job, it was time to make a change. I knew I needed to turn things around, and I knew what I needed to do to begin the process.

I made two phone calls; one was to GBP Live, a New York-based production company that would secure me for thirty to forty shows per year. The second call was to my contact that works for a top contracting firm based in Chicago. These were my two best bets to dig myself out from feeling irrelevant.

I had met on several occasions the owner and driving force behind GBP Live. My call to him was easy, unforced, and productive.

On to Chicago!

Up until now, I had only contacted the Chicago company via email. Since 2017 I have been contracting for them with great success. Part of my success, I believe, was based not only on the great product I was able to deliver but also my fees are substantially less than all of the competition. Reliable work and lower cost, along with my capabilities of negotiating multi-city orchestras, as I previously outlined, offered another checkmark in the "good" column for all producers.

Most contracting firms carry different fixed costs that need to be included in each bid on an event. Because I work from my home office, my fixed cost was the lowest imaginable: zero, apart from office supplies (paper, ink, etc.). I have no liability insurance, nor do I carry workers' compensation insurance. Those points allow me to operate at a lesser cost than my competitors.

For all of my contracting work, I secure a private payroll service to write all employee checks. The payroll company must have all the necessary insurances required by law to operate, including liability and workers' compensation insurance.

I secured a payroll company named Pro Music LLC. Pro Music charges me a set fee to run each payroll. By securing the company to act as my source of payroll, I, in turn, become an employee of Pro Music. Because I become an employee of Pro Music, they must file all contracts with each local union nationwide and assume all responsibilities, and liabilities, for all my work. I send invoices to the Chicago company, and they, in turn, wire the money directly to Pro Music. Using Pro Music is a big plus for me and the overall budget.

Years earlier, I closed my own company, Arts Alive International, Inc., due to IRS nonsensical issues. Those issues are discussed in my first book *Onward and Upward*, and I do not wish to relive that particular nightmare again!

My colleague Lars works as the Chicago coordinator, overseeing all United States productions. He and I had built a friendly relationship over the years, although I never actually spoke to him on the phone. Nonetheless, I dialed his number. Lars appeared to be stunned when he heard my voice on the other end of his phone receiver for the first time ever.

Once getting beyond the awkwardness of voice recognition, we made small talk for a few minutes before he asked me, "What's up?" I simply shared with him that I left my job of twenty-plus years and found myself with more time on my hands. Lars responded with, "well, I do believe we can add to your work schedule." Though I was incredulous, I shared that his response brought an optimistic smile to my face. Lars said, "Just you wait."

That was music to my ears, not only for the work, but because the response brought about a renewed dedication to what we Neglias do—live for the arts, for performance, for the music itself.

To this day, I cannot recognize if I ever crossed the line into depression, and if so, how close I might have come to my destruction. What I do know is that I never wish to experience boredom again.

After my chat with Lars, the dark hanging rain cloud passed under the ultraviolet rays of the intense sun. In a moment, the months of darkness were gone.

INTERLUDE: MEET MY GREAT-UNCLE

"You can't wait for life not to be hard before you can be happy" –The Author

Francesco Paolo Neglia studying his score –1914

Francesco Paolo Neglia was a native of Enna, Sicily. He was born on 22 May 1874, into a musical family. His father, Joseph, was a violinist and choirmaster at the local cathedral. His mother, Maria, was a primary school music teacher.

Francesco begged his father to enroll him in the conservatory of Palermo, but his parents could not afford to send him. As a result, he continued studying the violin and playing in his father's orchestral ensemble. In January 1890, Francesco began playing with the cathedral orchestra as a student violinist; this position carried a small stipend. It wasn't until 1893 that he became a full-time violinist. His pay went from an annual salary of £25 to £76.50. Simultaneously, Francesco earned his diploma as an elementary teacher at the Scuola Normale in Piazza Armerina. Obtaining his teacher certification allowed him the possibility to teach in public schools.

In 1894, Francesco applied to the Vincenzo Bellini Conservatory in Palermo with no success. All his attempts were in vain as he was over the age restriction. After a period of deep frustration, however, he managed to be interviewed by Maestro Guglielmo Zuelli. Zuelli recognized Francesco's talents and wanted to help him succeed. Thanks to Zuelli, Francesco was able to find a place as a first violinist in the orchestra of the Politeama Garibaldi. Once winning this position, for the first time, Francesco had economic stability and complete independence.

Additionally, Zuelli had accepted him as a private student giving him composition lessons without payment, and soon, Francesco became his favorite student. At the same time, Francesco completed his violin studies with Maestro Stroncone and piano studies with Maestro Carmelo Lo Re.

Maestro Guglielmo Zuelli at the time of his directorate
at the Conservatory of Parma –18 May 1914
photo credit Maurizio Agrò, *FP Neglia Nella vita e nell'arte*

A few years later, in 1897, Francesco won the position of concertmaster of the Teatro Massimo orchestra. Simultaneously, he obtained the position of Maestro of the conservatory as the assistant chair of Theory and Solfeggio. He was already writing numerous compositions and was beginning to make friends with other musical talents, such as Giuseppe Mule and Gino Marinuzzi. These early years proved to be very successful for young Francesco, as his music career was now grounded.

Between 1896 and 1898, Francesco composed his *Intermezzo breve* (1896) for symphonic orchestra, *Due Rispetti* (1898) for voice and piano, *Prayer* (1898), and a *Largo* (1898) for strings, harp, and organ, as well as a march for a large band, *Sfilata di Eroi* or *Parade of Heroes* (1896).

On 26 July 1896, Francesco conducted a performance of *a Lenno in Sant'anna* for choir and orchestra, and on Monday, 27 July 1896, the newspaper "Corriere dell'Isola" wrote: "We offer our warmest congratulations to Maestro Neglia for his beautiful composition in which we admired a great elegance of style, of the modern school, and a lot of sentiment."

The Dibbern family took an interest in the young musician and welcomed him first to their home as a guest and then as a teacher to their children. The head of the family had been a wealthy ship owner. His widow and his three children, Marie, Annie, and George were spending the summer in Palermo.

It didn't take long for a relationship with the eldest Dibbern to mature, and on 17 December 1900, at the age of 26, Francesco married Marie, whose family was of German descent. As a result of their marriage, Francesco came into contact with a fervent musical world and the best German symphony orchestras. Soon doors would open as he had the opportunity to manifest his formidable artistic and organizational energies with his new friends and acquaintances.

Francesco devoted the majority of his time to composition, writing the *Gloria in Excelsis Deo*, a fugue for five voices (circa 1900); *Symphony No. 1 in D minor (1901)*; two *Ave Maria's* (one dedicated to his wife, 1901); *Gavotte in G major*, for strings; and the *Minuet* in antique style, for strings (1900). Also, he met the poet Alessandro Cortella, and together they began drafting some scenes of the first act of Francesco's opera, *Zelia*.

Marie Dibbern, the first wife of Francesco Paolo –1900
photo credit Mario Barbieri's *FP Neglia, La Vita Le Opera*

Francesco's musical life came alive in the fall of 1901 when he moved to Hamburg. Maria's aunt, Anna Ahrens, met Francesco in Spies. Anna was an excellent musician herself as well as a cultured woman who introduced Francesco to the intellectual circles of Germany.

Anna Spies, Maria's aunt –1901
photo credit Mario Barbieri's *FP Neglia, La Vita Le Opera*

By 1903, Francesco conducted his first symphonic concert in Hamburg, but the critics did not accept his debut. It became abundantly clear that his Italian roots were not translating to his German audience. The critics wrote the word "crucify" in one of their reviews, claiming his interpretation was superficial and without substantial nuances.

Francesco conducting Beethoven's *Symphony No. 9*
with chorus and orchestra in Hamburg –10 February 1913
photo credit Mario Barbieri, *FP Neglia, La Vita Le Opera*

Encouraged by Zuelli, Francesco's valued mentor, he made the necessary adjustments. Additionally, Francesco had the good fortune to hear all of Beethoven's Symphonies performed by the Berlin Philharmonic Orchestra conducted by Artur Nikisch and by the Hamburg orchestra conducted by Max Fiedler and Richard Strauss. After hearing these groups perform, he understood that the Hamburg critics were not entirely wrong in unleashing their Teutonic wrath on him.

Francesco wrote in his 1903 journal the following:

"I shook myself, awakening from the lethargy, tirelessly studying this sublime music. I understand it after having assimilated it well. I came back with the Beethoven *Symphony No. 3, The Eroica,* which immediately resulted in the invitation to direct it in Kiel and to take it on a long tour throughout Germany."

Francesco was the first to organize "popular concerts" in Hamburg. He was excited to present a concert he conducted of Verdi's *Prelude to Sicilian Vespers* and Beethoven's *Symphony No. 5*. The public, and critics accepted the concert, which excited Francesco, who was now living beyond his dreams, as he gained city-wide recognition.

He also introduced to the German community some of his compositions, such as the *Fantastic Dance* (1902), *Largo for strings, harp, and harmonium* (1898), and the *Ave Maria* (1900), which baritone Signore Franck sang, accompanied on the harmonium by Signore Brodersen.

In many of his violin recitals he was accompanied on piano by Anna, who was enthusiastic about Francesco and greatly influenced him. The two spent a lot of time discussing music and studied scores together, often Italian music still unknown at the time in Germany.

Anna played an essential role in his success in Hamburg since she had many friends considered to be part of the high society. Even after Francesco returned to Italy in September 1914, their friendship lasted. They remained close up until Francesco died in 1932.

Francesco's success as a violinist and music teacher grew. Because he was in such high demand and had more student requests than he could handle, he surrounded himself with collaborators and founded a musical institute called Akademisches Musik-Institut.

With his access to so many students at the Akademisches Musik-Institut, he began to plan concerts. He wanted to showcase his talented students. On 31 March 1905, the Maestro organized his first major concert for his students at Conventgarten in Hamburg, Germany. The concert program included: Schumann's *Lullaby*; the first movement of a Mozart *Concerto* performed by Miss H. Steckmest; Beethoven's *Third Piano Concerto in C minor*, performed by Anna Ahrens, and Weber's *Third Piano Concerto in F minor* with Miss Hisekorn. It was a brilliant performance that was well-received by all.

As a result of the publics' desire to hear his music, and for those to have their children studying with the famous composer, his popularity grew exponentially. Due to this rapid influx of new students and Francesco's own desire, it was necessary to open two other branches of the Musik-Institut, in different districts of the city. The student enrollment exceeded five hundred students, and on 1 January 1908, the Institute was renamed The Neglia Conservatorium.

Francesco was no longer viewed as only a musician but also as an entrepreneur and an educator. He had refocused his energy towards the organization of concerts and the growth of his musical institute.

During the same period, he began his career as a conductor, leading to opportunities in Berlin, Kiel, Frankfurt, Main, and Bad Nauheim. He also served as an alternate with Felix Weingartner as the director of operas at the Hamburg State-Theater.

Negila Conservatorium, Stiftstraße 50, Hamburg
Germany. The school where Francesco Paolo and
his teachers taught over 500 students –1908
photo credit: Mario Barbieri, *FP Neglia, La Vita Le Opera*

On 6 October 1910, the well-known musical magazine "Signale für die Musikalische Welt" in Berlin defined him as one of the best interpreters of Beethoven's *Ninth Symphony*. His interpretation made history.

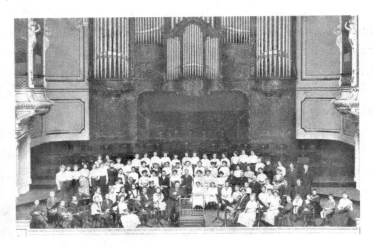

Francesco Paolo Conducting at Conventgarten
in Hamburg, Germany –1912
photo credit: Maurizio Agro *FP Neglia Nella vita e nell'arte*

On 26 October 1910, the famous music critic of the Hamburger Fremdenblatt, Heinrich Chevalier, wrote:

> Hamburg's musical life can no longer do without Professor Neglia's concerts which display the enthusiastic creative and executive talents at which he excels as an artist. Neglia's talents form an integral and essential part of the happy successes of our artistic events—both for the compilation of the programs and the execution.... Fidelity and respect for the work of art (Beethoven's *Ninth*) distinguishes Neglia above all, and leads him to an interpretation for which one desires nothing more. The choir performed with enthusiasm and with that confidence which overcomes all difficulties. Such confidence is full of conviction in one's merits and Neglia acts electrifyingly as a director of large forces.

Maestro Neglia was deservedly celebrated by those present with a succession of applause.

Regarding his conducting of Beethoven's symphonies, the distinguished critic Ferdinand Pfohl wrote in the "General Anzeinger" on 14 February 1914:

> Diligent directors are not those artists who rest comfortably on their laurels. Neglia proceeds vigorously with authentic artistic impulse and strives to improve his technique as director. He not only considerably penetrated the profound secrets and problems of Beethoven's titanic creation, but he also found the capacity to more and more refine his interpretation.... Today's performance was governed by such devout dedication that the sincerest acknowledgment cannot be denied, critical acclaim agreeing with the warm final ovations of the audience. The orchestra and choir were entirely under the inspirational influence of the conductor.

The positive, most radiant reviews continued to be printed for all to see. On 14 February 1912, Jacopo Napoli wrote in the "Hamburger Fremdenblatt":

> Professor Neglia directed both works, Beethoven's *First* and *Ninth* Symphonies, from memory. This certainly was not simple exhibitionism; in itself, it's empty of meaning. But to Neglia, who is opposed to any form of exhibition, it means something else. We can see his familiarity with the composition, which was reflected in the performance. Neglia displays his love of a foreigner at every moment and occasion the music spoke. Neglia delivers the essential Beethoven to us. And we are pleased to see how this tireless dedication

allows Neglia an ever-deeper understanding of the great musical creator and a limpid and clear delineation of the individual groups of thoughts in the symphonic poems of the beloved Maestro.

This gradual maturation did not make Neglia a sophisticated and pedantic musician; it will never make him such: because, on the contrary, he is an artist who above all has a heart, a musician extremely sensitive to all the beautiful and wondrous things of art. These traits allow Neglia's musical art the possibility of a warm, immediate sensitivity to be listened to even by a simple and loyal man. A man who has no other desire than to penetrate the heart of those in front of him [...] a performance that expressed the purest sentiment and impetuous enthusiasm and showed in the foreground a conductor in whose hands are all the threads of a great musical ensemble. The audience gave frantic applause for the enormous success of the unforgettable evening.

Francesco's calendar was filled with new and wonderful opportunities. They ran from 1908 right up until the death of his father in 1914.

Two highlights took place in 1910 when, in one performance, Francesco presented in a single concert, the ambitious *Hymnus* for mezzo-soprano and orchestra by Richard Strauss and the *Twardowsky Rhapsody* by Ferdinand Pfohl, and later that year, he conducted the entire cycle of 11 symphonies of Anton Bruckner.

In the wake of Wolf's and Mahler's lieder, he wrote a cycle of lieder himself for voices and orchestral accompaniment, the *Sechs Lieder im Volkston (1911)*, today unfortunately lost. Francesco may have written the Lieder in homage to Mahler, who died earlier that year. The fact is that on Mahler's death, many musicians paid him tribute; among them was Richard Strauss, a friend of Francesco.

This hypothesis arises from the fact that in 1912, Neglia composed the marvelous *Second Symphony*. It displayed a very Mahlerian character and style, highlighted in particular by using citations of popular songs.

There are no documents that prove with certainty the direct acquaintance between Neglia and Mahler. Still, Francesco himself said that to hear various performances of Beethoven's symphonies, he had to travel around Germany and had listened to several concerts. While attending these concerts, he met other musicians, and among them might have been Mahler, before Mahler's departure for New York in 1907.

Francesco achieved further success as world-famous soloists such as Teresa Carreño, Artur Schnabel, Ernestine Schumann-Heink, Arrigo Serato, Ugo Becker, and others participated in the concerts he directed.

The reviews were consistent, especially when it came to his interpretation of Bruckner. Regarding the execution of Bruckner's *Ninth Symphony*, on 15 February 1910, the newspaper "Die Hamburger Woche" wrote: "Professor Neglia has finally achieved the masterful execution of Bruckner."

On 1 February 1911, the "Hamburger Fremdenblatt" wrote: "Neglia's performance was strong, with a moving effect, sustained simultaneously by both considerable seriousness and understanding of the musical content and the spiritual moods placed in it. We must also accept the fact that Neglia has brought the southern temperament to our country of Germany, and in the most positive way."

Francesco completed his *Second Symphony in D minor* in 1912 and the symphonic suite *Three Paintings of Venetian Life* in July 1913. Meanwhile, the writing of his only opera, *Zelia,* continued, Francesco composing the second and third acts in 1914.

Francesco's life and career were in a place of contentment and financial wellness. Gratefully, Francesco was able to provide for his family a comfortable lifestyle. But the tides were about to change.

Giacomo Puccini, after a performance of *Madame Butterfly* in Hamburg 1913, pens a note to Francesco "To Maestro Fr Paolo Neglia, I will remember, Giacomo Puccini, Hamburg 4 08 1913."

Enrico Caruso, signed photograph to Francesco after a performance of *I Pagliacci* 1909 Hamburg, Germany photo credit Mario Barbieri, *FP Neglia, La Vita Le Opera*

The Who

"It's only after you lose everything that you're
free to do anything." –Chuck Palahniuk

Early in 2019, Live Nation announced The Who's upcoming tour.

The Who announcement read:

"Roger Daltrey and Pete Townshend unleash the combustible force that is The Who, with symphonic accompaniment! Produced by Live Nation, and in celebration of a new album, The Who's MOVING ON! tour will bring their indelible brand of powerhouse rock to North America, with special guests: Simon Townshend, guitar/vocals, Loren Gold, keyboard, Jon Button, bass and Zak Starkey on the drums."

A few weeks after reading the news, on 4 March 2019, an email from Lars with the subject titled *The Who orchestra tour - September* was sitting in my inbox. I had to reread the title several times before moving to the contents of the email. I was hoping I might get an offer, but just the thought of the possibility made my heart beat double-time. The company from Chicago approached me to bid on several performance dates on the upcoming tour.

I need to go back forty-five years to the mid-1970s when I was an impressionable 13-year-old to share with you what this opportunity meant to me. It was then that I first heard of The Who and drummer extraordinaire Keith Moon. From that day on, I knew two things. One was that when I grew up, I wanted to play the drums just like Moon; the other, I was listening to a band that would remain in my top few favorite groups of my lifetime.

16 years old, behind the drums –1979

Now, seated behind my computer, I navigated through dozens of saved template files needed to run an accurate budget. I pulled the payment rates from all local unions, which corresponded to the cities budgeting, and got to work. I learned that The Who orchestra required a magnificent 49 musicians, from violins and violas to woodwinds, brass, and percussion. As directed, I need to budget out a three-hour rehearsal and a three-hour performance along with a one-hour sound check. All services were to take place on the same day. Additionally, I calculated the pension payments and the required health benefits of each local union.

I wrote an email back to Chicago with a city-by-city breakdown of all costs with the budget proposal completed. I recall hitting the send button and releasing my numbers to the company that would accept or decline them. If rejected, I would have missed out on the one tour I would have booked for free—the very thought of working with The Who was already a done deal in my mind. I knew my numbers were solid, and the waiting was simply a formality. Or was it? My mind played tricks on me as I became obsessed with the opportunity to work with my childhood heroes.

A day or so later, I received an email requesting an updated budget. When tour requirements keep changing, a new budget is required with each change. This happened several times throughout the following few weeks, and I was beginning to lose hope that the producers would ever settle on the particulars of the tour. Still, I provided budgets with each request.

It wasn't until 18 March that the details of the show were pretty much grounded. After adjusting the budget, making sure all fees were accurate, I hit the send button for what I hoped to be the final time. All I needed to do now was wait.

On 22 March 2019, at 4:08 p.m., I received an email with the subject titled "WHO is a GO! plus a long list of musician requests" I was filled with happiness, my bid won, and I was about to work with a group of musicians I had grown up with and admired for more than forty years. After catching my breath and calming down, I shouted out loud, "We got it!" My wife, Sasha, ran to the room and kissed me with her congratulations.

Whenever a bid of mine was accepted, it wasn't only an opportunity for me to secure the musicians but also an opportunity for me to perform in the percussion section or as the orchestra's timpanist. It also allowed me to hire my worthy wife to lead the orchestra as concertmaster or principal of the second violin section. It was always a family affair as my work affected my wife and our living.

The tour ended up settling on 49 musicians in total. That meant I could secure 49 of my friends to play the shows, all of whom are highly qualified. There is no more incredible feeling I get than when I can offer musicians work, especially my friends. I was always thrilled to provide a good wage for an honest day's work. These were exceptionally high-profile shows, and I knew everyone in the industry would be as happy to play them as I was to contract them.

After calming down from the joyous news and allowing my heart to beat at a normal pace once again, I glanced back at the subject title to re-read it. The title stated, "plus a long list of musician requests." It was then I opened the attachment on the email. The attachment declared a complete list of musicians that I am to secure for each show. I had no choice but to comply, or the Chicago Company would use a contractor who would employ the music director's choice players.

Some are curious how musicians get added to my "hire" list. Generally speaking, I hear about other talented musicians from colleagues and conductor. Getting on my list by a solid reference is not the real challenge; staying on my list requires some doing, however. How does one remain on my hiring list? There is an easy answer to that question: don't be a jerk and impossible to work with; don't be needy; don't be unreasonable; don't make more work for me; be on time, smile, and as I like to say, play nice in the sandbox. That is the secret of getting and staying on my list.

When my group of regular freelance musicians learned I was booking the Who dates, they rushed to the Who website to see the dates. Most penciled the show dates into their agenda book before calling me. It crushed me when I wasn't able to make offers in my typical fashion. I needed to share with them that the music director had decided whom I will make work offers to. For me, a loyalist, this was a very new and painful process.

To mitigate potential issues with my colleagues, I decided to make my offer of work an all-or-nothing proposition. That means that each musician had to accept all the dates offered or none at all. Securing the same orchestra members for all the services helped me keep track of every aspect of the tour, as it can get very complicated to keep track of all the moving parts. I followed the music director's list to the letter and learned some of his requests were already obligated elsewhere during the requested dates.

Because I needed to provide musician lists to venues (there are heightened security concerns at all arenas), using the same musicians made my life easier. There were many moving parts that each musician was tied to; these included travel, payroll, union obligations, backstage lists, security badges, wrist bands, meal vouchers, holding areas, and a host of other issues that would pop up during the preparation process, as well as the unexpected, "onsite" issues. But the two that topped my list had to do with chartering buses and providing a consistent list of musicians for the music director.

As a contractor, when responsible for multiple dates, it is a bonus for the music director to learn the names of their players. Using the same musicians helps with making that task easier. So my idea of using all of the same players was ultimately agreed upon by the traveling music director (who happened to be a native New Yorker). I knew this would also please my payroll company, as they would, in the end, have less paperwork to process.

I would charter buses for all locations greater than 150 miles from a central location, such as Lincoln Center in Manhattan. I would assign and pay one of the orchestra members to be the bus captain; this would be a detail-oriented and meticulous person by nature. They would have a list of all personnel and ensure that all personnel were on the bus going to and coming from each performance on the road.

Using the same orchestra was a blessing in disguise as I soon learned that employing the "all or nothing" offer created a dozen openings from the music director's initial list of his requested musicians. A few were in the violin section, so my wife and a few of my closest, most talented musician friends were offered and ultimately secured for the tour.

When I left the New Jersey Symphony, only a few members reached out to me to share their dismay. There were only five besides my wife; no one else seemed to give a darn that I had left from my job. From that day forward, the dynamic five became closer friends; friends who we were able to lean on; friends who showed constant support; friends who had empathy and sincere concern for my and Sasha's well-being. To this day, we still get together to celebrate birthdays or just to celebrate life itself.

I learned that the shows set for September were moving up to May; I was caught off guard, to say the least! As a result, there was a lot of work to get done. At that time, I was in the midst of my orchestra season at the Jacksonville Symphony. These were exceedingly busy, but exciting, times, but for a spell I felt like I was drowning in details and emails. Although I wasn't convinced I would survive the deluge of details and actions needed to fulfill taking care of those details, I pressed on. As fate would have it, the September shows did not get canceled after all; they stayed in place, and the May dates were scheduled in addition to the fall dates. I felt like I just hit the lottery!

A few days after putting the spring and fall dates in place, I received a flurry of emails from my Chicago affiliate. The multiple emails included offers for other arena or large stage productions. The first was a budget request for the upcoming Game of Thrones tour; that show required 33 musicians, as the outfit carried many of its own traveling musicians. Although I had booked this tour before, I was happy to learn that Ramin Djawadi, the composer of the famed HBO series, would be conducting my leg of the tour. I was hopeful, and nearly sure, my bid would be accepted, as I had booked the past few tours for the same production.

I now had three tours: The Game of Thrones, Weird Al Yankovic's "Strings Attached" tour, and The Who tour. The flood gates opened, and my life became crazier and busier than it had been in the past 12 months.

A collection of security badges I collected
during a two-week period

If that was not enough to make me smile and feel grateful for the blessings bestowed upon me, another offer landed on my lap: a request for the Hugh Jackman tour, billed as "The Man. The Music. The Show." Getting fired from the New Jersey Symphony never felt so good!

For each of the offers from Chicago, I went through the exact process I did with all my shows. I meticulously prepare budgets, submit them, and ultimately win each bid. My life suddenly took on an entirely new dimension, that of a true North American music coordinator. I had been contracting for decades, but not on this level.

Early on in my career, I made a deal with myself, one I have stuck to all these years. I would never plead for work or make cold calls. I certainly didn't object to informing an organization that I would be happy to work with them on a project, but I never actively solicited contracting work. I always felt that to obtain success, it should come in a very organic, unforced way. Both sides mutually agree to move forward, with no secret backroom deals to be made.

Through my contact at GBP Live in New York, I met my Chicago counterparts, about as organic a manner as one can get, a solid referral. As a result of good old-fashioned blood, sweat, and tears, my career finally arrived in a place, up until now, I could only imagine.

The morning of the first Who tour date, I woke up with one all-consuming thought; today is the day I will share the stage with Roger and Pete from the Who.

I spent the better part of the morning thinking about what I would ask them if the opportunity arose. I kept coming back to the overwhelming feeling that they had probably heard every possible question in the universe. With that in mind, I began to think about which of their albums were at the top of my favorite list. Was it *Quadrophenia, Tommy, Who Are You, Who's Next, Live at Leeds,* or another? All worthy competitors, but I settled on an album they put out back in 1975, *The Who by Numbers.* The songs on the album were, for the most part, more introspective and personal than many other songs that the band had released, and I was drawn to them for my own personal reasons.

If given a chance, I might share how much I enjoyed the songs on that recording and how they impacted me at such a young age. When this album was released, I was just 12 years old and very impressionable.

I am always mindful that those with a celebrity status are sometimes not as chatty as we might wish. I have worked with many recognizable names in the industry and have learned a great deal about keeping my distance. Especially in my position, as the one in charge of the musicians, and has a path forward to say hello to an artist, I am acutely aware of keeping my distance unless I feel, without question, the door is open.

When I first worked with Johnny Mathis, I kept to myself, but shortly after the rehearsal concluded, Johnny himself approached me to offer thanks for lining up so many of his New York friends in the band. I received the same reaction from Yo-Yo Ma, Bernadette Peters, Hans Zimmer, and many others. Although some of the friendlier artists would acknowledge me in my position, others, who shall remain nameless, looked down their long, arrogant noses at me. I was just the hired hand to them. I pass no judgment on those who built a wall between us but feel that they are missing out on another side of the business, that of genuine camaraderie.

There were a few times where I couldn't figure out who was open and who wasn't, but those instances were few and far between. When I met the music director for the Who, it represented one of those uncertain times. I should start by saying that he is a great guy, very professional, and with a sophisticated understanding of our industry.

My very first Who rehearsal was set to begin shortly. All the musicians were on stage, noodling around on their instruments. All are in place, on time, and ready to go. The first part of our rehearsal was for the orchestra only; no band members were to attend.

A few minutes later, the music director entered the stage and took his place on the oversized waiting podium. I approached to introduce myself and thank him for having me contract so many of the shows on the schedule. He met me with a smile. When I shared with him where the orchestra needed to take their break, he gave me a sideways glance but with a smile. Then he shared that the Who had only two prior tour shows, and that things were constantly changing. He also said, not to worry, as he had a complete understanding of the structure of the rehearsals and performance in New York. He looked at me with the confidence and professionalism that any contractor would be thrilled to receive. Our relationship, both professionally and personally, progressed nicely.

After the three-hour orchestra rehearsal was over and the musicians were placed on break, the real fun was about to begin. A little background on large venues such as Madison Square Garden and the like: there is less room backstage than one might expect. For this tour, separate dressing rooms are required for each band member; the music director, backup singers, additional band members, touring manager, production offices, security offices, and if that wasn't enough, a large holding area was needed for the 49 musicians performing with the Who.

Additionally, food and beverage services require many workers due to more extensive food preparations and the additional serving needs in the dining areas. The tour feeds all staff, as it is cheaper to provide hot meals than a food stipend for the hundreds of people involved.

About 40 minutes before the scheduled soundcheck for the band itself, I was patiently waiting when I heard the rumblings of a motor approaching. Mind you, we were a few levels down from the street, in the belly of the Garden. If you think you hear a car motor, you most likely don't need to adjust your hearing; it is for real.

Coming down from the upper level was a giant van, an Escalade. Is that Tony Soprano? The car pulled to the underground entrance of the venue. Seconds later, the engine went silent; the door opened, and out came Roger Daltrey. My eyes nearly popped out of my head. One of my childhood heroes was standing just feet away from me. I was utterly blown away.

Roger got out of the car and headed to pass through the metal detector; once he did, he was escorted to his dressing room. I just wanted to run over to say hello, but I knew that could be a big mistake. Imagine I screw things up so severely that my Chicago folks have to beat me senseless! I controlled myself, but it wasn't easy.

The Escalade pulled away just in time for a limousine to exchange spots. I knew exactly who was in the limo. Once the door opened, my thoughts were confirmed. It was the legendary singer-songwriter Pete Townshend. This was the guy who wrote the rock opera *Tommy* and later *Quadrophenia*; he wrote "Baba O'Riley," "Won't Get Fooled Again," "Behind Blue Eyes," and dozens of other masterpieces.

Within ten minutes, the two original members of the Who were heading to the stage. Already in place were drummer Zak Starkey, bassist Jon Button, and a crew of others, one of which was singer-songwriter and guitarist, Simon Townshend, Pete's brother. I ran out to the audience area to listen to the band's soundcheck. Waiting with excitement, the group started, and when they did, I could barely control myself. My emotions were running away from me.

Since the early eighties, I had been offered concert tickets to see The Who with my brother John and friends. I always had conflicts with my symphonic life and turned down the chance to see my favorite band. In all the years of me loving the band, up until now, I had never seen them live. If I saw only the soundcheck, I would be completely content, but there was more to come.

The band rehearsed and warmed up to "I Can See for Miles" and "Who Are You" for roughly twenty minutes. They were all adjusting their volume levels in their ear monitors and the levels of their instruments. It was fascinating to observe, and I loved every minute of their process.

Pete and Simon Townshend's guitars located stage left at
Madison Square Garden –May 2019

After their brief soundcheck, the band broke, and it was now time for me to call the 49-piece orchestra back to the stage for the tutti rehearsal: the orchestra, and the band together for the first and only time before the evening performance. The full sound check was slated for 60 minutes, 50 minutes of playing time, and 10 minutes for a break.

During the many soundchecks I've attended over the years, I've often found an out-of-the-way place on stage to observe the proceedings. Today, I found myself sitting center stage, just behind one of the backup singers, but with a complete view of what was before me.

Soundcheck, I was sitting close enough to touch them.

The music director started conducting the overture from *Tommy*, and before I knew it, Pete was playing full force no more than 10 feet away from me. Roger was about six feet away, just to the right of Pete. My rock and roll idols were within arm's reach, and I found myself completely overwhelmed with happiness and fulfillment. I remember thinking, precisely at that moment, if this were the last thing I ever contracted in my career, I would be satisfied, as I have experienced the absolute best of the best.

I panned the stage from right to left, watching my colleagues perform, the Who singing and playing, and my new acquaintance, the music director, swinging away. I was grateful to be the one who helped put it all together. That is self-gratification, the feeling of accomplishment, success, and contentment. My life had come full circle; that is how I felt. From the days I learned how to hold drum sticks to the days I understood how to interact and work with others, all roads led me to this day. Here I stand, in the middle of complete astonishment.

As the soundcheck came to a close, I found myself glued to my seat on the stage. It was then that the music director called me to the podium. I rose to answer his needs. Once his question was answered, I began heading back to my place on stage. It was then that Pete called me over and said, "So you are the local contractor responsible for putting this great orchestra together. I cannot thank you enough for helping us out." He extended his hand, and I grabbed it in recognition.

I thanked him and told him how happy I was to finally meet the person who wrote so many tunes that made me happy. Pete said, "Oh, which one or ones do you like?" I was prepared! "Apart from your brilliant writing on *Quadrophenia*, and so many other albums, I adore all the tunes on *The Who by Numbers*, including 'Blue, Red, and Grey.'" Pete smiled with understanding, which in turn made me smile.

I also thanked him for scoring their music, which normally would consist of guitars, bass, drums, and keyboards for a 49-piece symphonic orchestra. I shared with him that as a contractor, one of my greatest joys is to employ musicians from city to city, throughout the country. Pete acknowledged my excitement which was clearly visible in my smile and enthusiastic chat. Not wanting to overstay my welcome, I thanked him again for his music and conversation. It was now time to dismiss the orchestra. I went to the dinner area to decompress from the past hours' events.

Little did I know that during my short conversation with Pete, the timpanist, a friend of mine, snapped several photographs on his phone. A few minutes after my conversation ended, my phone, tucked in my back pocket, began to vibrate. When I pulled it out to see what problem I needed to solve, I was stopped in my tracks.

Jim and Pete. A lifelong dream fulfilled.

We had a few hours between the soundcheck and performance. Tens of thousands of people were filling the hall, and I was intoxicated thinking about my exchange with Pete and in anticipation of the show to come.

I was pacing, practically walking in circles, just waiting for the first of several shows to begin. Having an "all-access" badge, I learned I could go wherever I wished; I could go backstage where the stars were, I could walk to the front of the stage in the private area, with no one to stop me. It was terrific, and I must say, I felt enlightened!

In one of my circles backstage, I literally bumped into Roger Daltrey in front of his dressing room door. I greeted him with a hello and a short introduction of who I was. He told me, "Chap, I know who you are from the rehearsal, but it is nice to meet you." I chuckled and thanked him for having me as his contractor. I then told him the timpanist for the tour was the husband of an actress who performed with Roger during his run of "A Christmas Carol" at Madison Square Theater back in 1998. Roger lit up like a pile of fireworks! He held me by the shoulders and shared with me that he struggled with his voice during that run of shows. He asked my friend's wife if she had a doctor who could help him, and she did. A relationship was built.

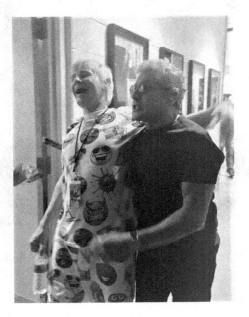

Drummer Zak Starkey and Roger walking
to the stage before the show.

All the time, I was thinking to myself, I am chatting with Roger Daltrey, the guy who recorded the vocals on "Love Reign O'er Me." I was fulfilled, gratified, and content with the day, fully knowing that we had many more shows together in the future. I was on cloud nine.

At the risk of offending Roger, I asked if he wouldn't mind sharing a photograph with me. Without hesitation, he agreed. When I went to take a selfie with him, he stopped and said, "No, we deserve better," and called one of the security guards over. That guard snapped this photograph on my iPhone.

Roger and Jim, after a rehearsal

Between the conversations with Roger and Pete and the two photographic memories to add to my life's work, I was as content as I had ever experienced in my life. Although the first performance was now in the books, I was already thinking about the performances yet to come. And about the next tour, which was scheduled to take place in the fall.

After completing this chapter and reflecting on the joy and sense of euphoria, I felt one of my favorite quotes could best sum up how I felt working with The Who.

"I don't regret that the ride has to be over, but rather feel grateful for the miles I have traveled, for the sights along the way, and to be exactly where I am." –Neil Peart

Sold-out performance at Madison Square Garden,
NYC. During the first half of the performance, I went
to the upper seats to snap this photograph.

COLLEAGUES

"My soul is a hidden orchestra; I know not what instruments, what fiddle strings and harps, drums and tamboura I sound and clash inside myself. All I hear is the symphony." –Fernando Pessoa

In August 2018, I received a phone call from a colleague. It had been at least 15 years since we spoke. Upon my "hello," we quickly moved to the thrust of the call. The General Manager and Vice President of operations of the Jacksonville Symphony Association called to ask questions about personnel managing in the most general sense. Knowing him for so long, we picked up a thread of conversation which began some 15 years ago.

The call concluded after answering some questions about a personnel manager's duties. What I couldn't have imagined was what happened shortly after that call. Around mid-September, my colleague requested I come down to Jacksonville. He was inviting me to take an interim position as the personnel manager with the orchestra. They needed someone with experience and understanding of the position to come in while they began their search to replace the outgoing personnel manager.

My wife and I discussed the offer and considered it from many angles. Although I was freelancing with many companies, including my Chicago team as music coordinator, I yearned for the daily hustle I enjoyed when I held my orchestra personnel manager position in New Jersey. This position comes with a fixed schedule, dates, times, rehearsal orders, and performances. Sasha and I had a lot to consider, time away from our sons, salary, time apart, and so much more. Both of us knew, deep down, that this was an excellent opportunity. I knew my soul needed this particular nourishment, the food of a symphony orchestra.

After a conversation with my colleague, we worked out fair compensation and other terms of my initial 18-day stay in Florida. My colleague wanted me to start on 1 October 2018, but I had an unavoidable conflict with that date, an 8 p.m. performance at the Wells Fargo Arena in Philadelphia with the Han Zimmer tour on October 2. I had guaranteed the presenters that I would personally attend the date. Ultimately, we agreed that I would begin at 10 a.m. on 3 October.

I had booked a handful of east coast dates for the Zimmer tour, and this was the last of the shows on my run. The Zimmer show ran for 2 hours 28 minutes; it would let out at 10:28 p.m. That meant I would arrive back at our New Jersey home no earlier than 12:30 a.m. With a 6 a.m. flight booked, it was going to be a short night.

On 3 October, at 8:45 a.m., flight 2343 landed at JAX International Airport. After disembarking the aircraft and gathering my oversized piece of luggage, I exited the airport and got my first taste of Jacksonville. It was already a staggering 85 degrees and heading up to a high of 93. For this northern boy, it was warm, and I felt it.

Upon the airplane tires hitting the tarmac in Florida, my purpose came into complete focus. No matter how tired I was, in about 75 minutes, I would be standing in front of an orchestra for the first time in 12 months. Although I had spent more than 30 years doing my gig, today felt different; my emotions were heightened.

I took an Uber to 300 Water Street, home of the Jacksonville Symphony Association. The symphony has a 10 a.m. rehearsal, and I was to begin my short stint with the orchestra just an hour after landing. As we pulled up to the Times-Union Center for the Performing Arts front door, I snapped into my present, professional mode, not that of the past. At that exact moment, I knew the past was over, and the future was lying just feet away from the idling Uber.

The driver dropped me off at the hall's security entrance; I grabbed my luggage and entered the building. When I arrived at the security desk, I was greeted by Sergeant Hogan, head of security for the Times

Union-Square facility. She greeted me with, "You must be Jim Neglia." I smiled, and although exhausted, confirmed my identity.

Sergeant Hogan buzzed me in and pointed me in the right direction. Before I could step more than ten feet, my old friend and colleague greeted me with the enormous smile and professionalism that would solidify his position with the organization. It was great to see him after all these years.

I was directed to the personnel manager's office, which is on the same floor as the stage. It was now 9:40 a.m. and the rehearsal was set to begin in 20 minutes. My emotions were raw, as I had not performed as a musician or stood in front of an orchestra as a personnel manager to state the phrase "can we tune, please" in over a year. I wasn't nervous but I did feel a bit out of place or rusty.

Part of the orchestra personnel manager's duties is to ensure all services' timelines are followed to the letter. Starting a service on time means literally just that, on time. Imagine standing next to the conductor's podium, in front of 70 musicians, all of whom are warming up on their instruments. At the appointed time, I have to have the orchestra stop and be silent so that they can hear the tuning note "A" by the principal oboe.

I want to do my best to share the process with anyone who has not experienced this. Musicians fill the stage before the start of a service. They arrive and enter the stage anywhere from 9:00 to 9:45 a.m. and collectively start playing whatever works for them to limber up. They could play scales or parts of the music they are about to perform at the rehearsal or excerpts from other works.

When the clock strikes 10 a.m. precisely, the concertmaster stands. When the concertmaster stands, that signals the orchestra to stop warming up and listen for the "A" coming from the principal oboe.

On the stage, there is a clock that displays seconds as well as minutes and hours. When I ask the concertmaster to stand and tune, my attention moves to the clock that sits just above the stage. As I watched, I noted it took the orchestra 37 seconds to calm down, so the oboe could sound the A. Thirty-seven seconds was a very long time to wait, and I knew this was one of the first things that I would address.

Once the rehearsal began, I made my way to the personnel manager's office, booted up the waiting laptop, and sent the following email to the orchestra stating the obvious. It read something like this: "Dear Orchestra members, I would like to remind you that our rehearsals begin promptly at 10 a.m., please be prepared to tune precisely at 10 a.m."

The following morning, we had another 10 a.m. rehearsal. I acted exactly as I did the day before; at 10 a.m., I asked the concertmaster to tune the orchestra. This time, within seven seconds, there was silence on the stage, and within 35 seconds, the entire ensemble had tuned up. It took less time than just 24 hours earlier. This simple accomplishment made me feel that I could make a difference in Florida.

It is always tricky to walk into a new environment, where an orchestra has its own culture, habits, and rhythm. Generally, it is not wise for the new kid on the block to come in and make significant changes.

After the rehearsal started, I spent my second day sorting through endless emails unattended to by my predecessor. There was a total of 186 unanswered emails waiting in the inbox. By the time I answered the waiting emails on October 4 and 5, most of the requests, or information, were past due. This meant that they had been in the personnel manager's email box for at least four weeks. This would never happen in my world, as I have made it my absolute policy to answer all emails in my inbox within 24 hours. Although some of my responses might be, "I am not sure, but I am looking into it," at least the person writing will receive a response. I needed to answer emails to people in positions which I was unfamiliar with. I didn't know who was who; this made my work challenging early on. Before answering an email, I needed to research who was writing, what instrument they play and position, the rules of our CBA (collective bargaining agreement), and how to help them.

I would receive a simple email such as, "I would like to take leave from the orchestra on such and such day," prompting me to read the collective bargaining agreement, so I can either accept or decline their request. Additionally, each musician was entitled to only a certain amount of paid or unpaid leave. I needed to find their file and make decisions based on each individual's criteria. It was a mess, and I was working on an enormous learning curve.

I worked 18-hour days for the first two weeks I was in Jacksonville. Thank goodness, I was staying across the street from the hall at the Omni Hotel. During that time, the only time I would go back to the hotel was to sleep. The downside is 18 days in a hotel made for a miserable existence. I did not want to eat all my meals at the hotel; a breakfast buffet and a late-night dinner was a recipe for disaster, at least for me.

I raised my concern with my colleague, and he called the Omni to request some additions. To make my life a bit more palatable, the Symphony arranged for a large refrigerator and microwave to be added to my room. Those two accommodations proved to be very helpful.

Daily, I would wake, early—very early—as I watched the rising sun seep through the half-open shades in my 16th-floor room. As my eyes opened, I would spring out of bed, no matter the time, and start my day. Watching the sunrise over the sea of bridges covering the Saint Johns River was invigorating.

Checking my larger supplied refrigerator in my room, I would take a pack of pre-cooked hard-boiled eggs, along with the waiting glass of orange juice and coffee that were sitting on the other side of my locked door. I would place an order each night that would hang on my door handle, waiting to be filled by the Omni's attentive workers.

The unfortunate side of my Jacksonville stay was that I had no car. The plus side was that the Omni offered excellent service to their patrons, a driver named Phil. Phil was on call during certain hours, and I could call on him to take me to and from various locations. One of my favorite trips was to the Fresh Market, an establishment about a mile away. Sometimes, I would walk from the Omni along the beautiful river to the Fresh Market and call Phil to take me back with my groceries and wine. Unlike most New Jersey outlets, one of Florida's benefits is that alcohol is available at most supermarkets, gas stations, and convenience stores.

The next few weeks were simply a repeat of what took place the day before. One significant difference was that I had worked through all the emails and had begun settling all the issues with the membership. While doing so, I learned about those who worked in the operations department of the symphony. These folks were ultimately my lifeline. I always believed that the operations department must be closely united to run a successful, tight ship.

I immediately felt the support of all in the operations department. Their embrace offered me affirmation in my position and helped solidify our relationships, both in and out of the work environment. I was grateful to be part of such a multifaceted team, a team that made me feel at home.

Although I had only 18 days with the organization, every one of them felt comfortable and special. I thought I had been offered a unique opportunity to revisit my old life and use that experience as a springboard to the future.

HUGH JACKMAN

"Success usually comes to those who are too busy to be looking for it." –Henry David Thoreau

Dress rehearsal, Madison Square Garden –2019

The spectacular set for Act I, Madison Square Garden –2019

"Academy Award*-nominated, Golden Globe- and Tony Award-winning performer Hugh Jackman, with AEG Presents and TEG-Dainty, presents The Man. The Music. The Show. World tour! Featuring a live orchestra and including hit songs from The Greatest Showman, Les Misérables, The Boy from Oz, and more from Broadway and film!"

When the call came in to book the Hugh Jackman shows, I first needed to google Hugh Jackman, as I knew him only as a movie actor, not in any other industry area. I soon learned that Mr. Jackman was billed as the "greatest showman." I would later discover he earned the title. I read more to learn all about this multifaceted and enormously talented man. He was a movie actor with a large following; he is billed as a singer, stage actor, and producer.

I was offered four back-to-back shows at Madison Square Garden in New York; two performances at the Wells Fargo Center in Philadelphia; one at the Nassau Coliseum in Long Island; and one at the Prudential Center in Newark, New Jersey. I couldn't wait to bid and win these productions.

A request for a budget from these large arena-size productions looks something like this (my comments are in italics):

Please provide a budget based on the criteria listed below.

Hugh Jackman: The Man. The Music. The Show.
ORCHESTRA SPECIFICATIONS – updated 30 May 2019
These shows are one-off, arena-style concert presentations.

Unless you know it's covered for sure, please assume that free parking will not be provided and allow for that cost in your estimate.

Many local unions require parking reimbursement as part of their collective bargaining agreement.

Show Day SCHEDULE (subject to adjustment)

Bear in mind that all of this could change; I follow the outline as requested on the day sent.

Bearing in mind that service length restrictions vary, please advise us on the most cost-efficient way to cover this production schedule in your location. One rehearsal, plus one 1-hour soundcheck; please budget up to three hours for the rehearsal.
Rehearsal lengths are generally 2½ hours, not three, so the budget will increase at their request.
Note that, due to venue load-in and stage building needs, there may not be a lot of flexibility in the following Show Day Schedule:

12 p.m. – 3 p.m. Orchestra rehearsal - Offstage
3 p.m. – 4 p.m. Break
4 p.m. – 5 p.m. Sound-Check

7:15 p.m. Official Orchestra Performance Start Time.

The tickets to the public read, 7 p.m., but the orchestra's call was fifteen minutes later. This was to accommodate latecomers, which would push the actual start time to the stated. If we start at 7 p.m., we must conclude at 9:59:59 p.m. or go into overtime and incur more charges. The Jackman show, I imagined, must have been close to the three-hour mark.

Need a 3-hour Performance Call (Please remind me: is a 2.5-hr call available?).

Generally, all performances in nearly every local union fall within the 2.5-hour call. Once we move past the 2½ hour time period, we move into overtime in 15-minute increments. This is all part of the overall budget and needed to be included in the bid.

INSTRUMENTATION (supplemental local musicians)

UPDATED 5/30/19

Woodwind I - Alto Saxophone, Flute, Piccolo, and Bb Clarinet
Woodwind II - Alto Saxophone, Tenor Saxophone, Flute, Bb Clarinet
Woodwind III - Tenor Saxophone, Bb Clarinet, Oboe, and English Horn
Woodwind IV - Baritone Saxophone, Bb Clarinet, Bass Clarinet, optional Bassoon

Optional Additional Woodwind V - dedicated Oboe/English Horn (only - eliminates oboe/EH on Woodwind III chair)
Optional Additional Woodwind VI - dedicated Bassoon (only - eliminates bassoon on the Woodwind IV chair)"
The woodwind requirements are very specific and require precise calculations. If a Woodwind 1 is hired to play just one instrument, they will receive a salary based on that instrument. When you start adding additional instruments, you must compensate the player to cover the remaining requirements. Those additional instruments each carry an additional fee or "double." Looking at Woodwind 1, they would receive 100% of salary

for alto saxophone, 20% additional for flute, 10% additional for piccolo, and 10% more for Bb clarinet; a total of 140% or 40% over scale.

That percentage of an overpayment would also impact the pension contributions. If 16.25% pension is part of the agreement, that needs to be calculated and entered for all doublings—that comes to 140% over scale. I applied the same philosophy to all woodwind players.

BRASS: The brass players should be more Broadway-style, with a strong lead trumpet.

This means the player was not solely an orchestral musician but versatile in many areas, especially the style of Broadway. A "strong lead trumpet" refers to soloistic qualities and one who can play in the higher range of the instrument.

Three trumpets, one tenor trombone, one bass trombone, one percussionist/timpanist.

For the percussionist/timpanist, they were looking for one player capable of covering a plethora of percussion instruments and mastery behind the timpani.

All percussion equipment provided by tour – Please peruse the Percussion Folder at the link shown below.

STRINGS: Two violins, one viola, one cello.

**Musicians are requested to bring portable music stands for the off-stage rehearsal.

This was to help facilitate a rehearsal in one area while the performance stage was being set. There would not be portable stands on stage, but concert, heavy-duty professional music stands for the members.

SHEET MUSIC - PDFs available for download at <u>this link</u>.

This would allow the musicians to prepare the music before the rehearsal and performance.

** Hard copies will travel with the tour. You are not required to print the parts.**

** You will see three trombone folders in the sheet music repository. The tour has requested two trombones. The 2nd trombone folder contains parts that reach down into the bass trombone range. We are not sure how the 2nd and 3rd trombone parts will be distributed within a single folder. We are requesting one tenor and 1 bass trombone.**

ATTIRE: Show blacks (head to toe black clothes). No costumes.

OTHER: Sheet music, stands, lights, chairs, and percussion provided by the tour.

That was a lot to digest and prepare, but just as I do for all productions, I started to dissect the needs of the tour and run the numbers according to each local union's requirements.

As I experienced during the Who tour, the music director had his top choices for all orchestra positions. All of his choices were those who had worked with Jackman in New York years earlier. Unfortunately, this caused a lot of turmoil for those I had hired for gigs over the years.

Many of them couldn't wrap their heads around the fact that my hands were tied. It was on this particular tour I learned who my real friends were; I also realized that there were very few of them to speak of. My life consisted of offering work to others, which set off a chain of events. I would offer work; they would pretend to be faithful, loyal friends. But as I have shared in the Who chapter, my real friends were limited to the five from my past job. A real-life lesson was learned during this tumultuous time.

My bid was accepted, again and again. I was on a roll, and the Chicago company knew that I was an honest, hard-working music coordinator that just wanted to work and enjoy life.

All the contractors employed by the Chicago company, to cover the entire United States dates, were instructed, "Do not bother Mr. Jackman for photographs or selfies. Please inform the musicians." When the company sends out such a warning, there is no question that the warning must be followed.

Once all negotiations with the local unions were in place, all contracts were signed, and the orchestra was hired, there was nothing to do but wait for the actual performance dates. The first of the shows was slated for 30 June 2019, at the Wells Fargo Center in Philadelphia.

Backstage at the Wells Fargo Arena, Pennsylvania
–30 June 2019

Upon entering the venue, it was hard not to notice the enormous spectacle on the stage. The setting was something that was out of the ordinary; it was excessively ornate and eye-catching. Draping either side of the stage were 40-foot banners of Jackman in various roles. Stage right was a picture of him dressed as the Wolverine, and stage left was an image of the Australian with his shirt open, showing off his fantastic physique. Soon, there would be 20,000 screaming fans filling the empty seats enjoying what was before my eyes.

Jackman at the Wells Fargo Arena, curtain call!

Just like the Who set up, the orchestra rehearsed first without Mr. Jackman. The orchestra size was considerably smaller than that of the Who and Weird Al, so I was curious how the ensemble would sound. I was about to hear that the orchestrations are all carefully crafted, and the sound was enormous.

This was a large production where every aspect of the production team was at the highest level attainable. The lighting was engaging; the sound engineer was top-notch; the singers, dancers, and entire entourage were all at the industry's highest entertainment levels. I share this, even after working in the industry for over thirty-five years.

The excitement in me began to rev up in anticipation of the headliner, adding his charisma to the mix. I couldn't help but think that I was in for a real treat. Not only a musical treat but the complete entertainment experience of what was billed as "The Greatest Showman."

Jackman addressing the orchestra

Jackman appeared without warning. As he hit the stage, as you might imagine, there was excitement in the air. I had heard about the kindness of Jackman from various people who had been working with him on tour, but what I was about to witness over the next few hours and during every show I attended was astounding.

Upon taking the stage for the rehearsal, Jackman had a three- to four-inch stack of scratch-off lottery tickets in his hand. As he crossed from stage left to stage right, passing each of the musicians, he would pause in front of them and hand off a few tickets. It wasn't just the act of handing out the tickets, as much as it was the joy that was showering all over him and the stage personnel itself. Hugh had a way about him that I had rarely seen before, warmth and calm interwoven with an air of professionalism that was, up until that time, for this writer, unparalleled.

Hugh saying hello to friends from New York who were in the orchestra

I took an out-of-the-way seat behind the string section to observe, as I was accustomed to doing on all my bookings. Jackman motioned to me to stand and accept his gift of lottery tickets. I blushingly obliged. I kept thinking about this remarkable person who shared his enthusiasm and evident love of his art with all who were around.

After the rehearsal concluded, I dismissed the orchestra and showed them the way to their waiting hot dinner. All of the meals were supplied by the tour. I bumped into some of the same security guards that I met at some of my earlier Who dates. We chatted for a bit, shared some stories, then, in a blink, continued on our way.

My badge for this production was almost unlimited, unlike the Who tour, which was complete without limit. The one limitation placed on me was that I was not permitted to go beyond a specific point, where Jackman's dressing room was. I was already told not to bother Mr. Jackman by my Chicago firm, and I had no plans to do otherwise.

My backstage pass

Every single Jackman performance was a professional display of one hundred percent entertainment. These shows took entertainment to another level, to a place that the attendee would bring home as a once-in-a-lifetime experience. I was proud to play my part in the production, and my bosses in Chicago were growing happier and happier with their northeastern contractor. Life was good, and I was having more fun than I had ever imagined.

Part of the Jackman magic was his absolute caring for his colleagues. For example, fifteen minutes before every performance, he would gather the roughly 50 entertainers who would accompany him on stage for a meaningful group message. The message always had to do with the love and respect he had for all. Then he recognized some of the singers in the circle with a *"we are in this together"* message.

I would find somewhere inconspicuous to witness the same gathering that took place before every performance. I found it truly remarkable that with all that was going on, the pressure of a live performance, the needed concentration, the countless numbers that would share the stage, Jackman took the time to center his team and share a peaceful moment.

A moment of prayer, reflection, and love
backstage before every performance

For all the fun I was having, it didn't come without putting in a great deal of preparatory work or dealing with any on-site issues that might arise. As with all of my work, I felt responsible for everything that fell under my watch. This tour was no different, and there were issues; some were easy to resolve, and others, not so much.

On the final date of the tour, we did have one of those episodes. This particular episode was entirely out of my hands. The dismay came directly from the music director, and he expected me to resolve it.

Many people travel on tour with the authority to make decisions based on the level of their position. Sometimes the question of who is making the decisions and who is not hovers over a very blurry line, however. Before entering a new tour, I seek out the hierarchy within the touring company; this way, I deal with only one point-person, covering my backside on any possible conflicts.

I believe because I had been at each of the Jackman shows, my familiar face was one that some grew to rely on. In the long run, that is viewed as a positive attribute, but it could cause a ripple effect if misconstrued, landing me in hot water with my compatriots in Chicago.

After a somewhat uncomfortable mishap, I went into personnel manager mode and decided to document the occurrence.

Here is a recap of the episode which took place on 8 October 2019, at the Prudential Center in Newark, New Jersey.

On Sunday, I arrived at the Prudential Center two hours before the soundcheck. I was met by the local project manager, Paul, who gave me explicit directions not to allow the musicians near the catering, not even for coffee, and that water would be provided in the musicians' dressing room.

At 6:26 p.m., I received a text from the music director, who questioned why the musicians weren't permitted to go to catering. I shared with him what I was informed by Paul.

By 6:38 p.m., the music director had texted again, stating that the big boss, Daniel Rite, confirmed that the musicians could go to catering; in his words, "it is in the budget."

Unfortunately, all the musicians were eating outside the arena and the performance was set to start at 7:30 p.m. The music director was not happy at all and asked me to come to his dressing room.

At 6:44 p.m., I called the Chicago office to share what took place. The following day, the music director sent an email to the Chicago staff:

To paraphrase, it went something like this:

I want you to be aware of what happened on Sunday night. The Newark orchestra was told that they were not allowed to have dinner or even coffee catering. This was very embarrassing to both Hugh and me. We know all the musicians personally, and many have played with Hugh for many years. He even mentioned during the show how grateful he was that they were there.

I then checked with management, and they were supposed to have had dinner. Not sure how or why this happened, but I wanted to let you know how upsetting this was to me.

As you can see, this wasn't life-threatening or intentional at all, yet the incident escalated to a level where I was called to the music director's office via text.

Having a restricted access badge, I wouldn't be able to go to the music director's room, as it was right next to Hugh Jackman's dressing room. To gain access, I shared the music director's text with the attending guard. After reading it, he gave me entry to the corridor, which leads to the inner sanctum of the dressing rooms. I walked very quickly as I could feel the music director's agitation and frustration and wished to resolve the issue.

Head down, plowing down the hallway. I ran head-on into an individual. That individual was Hugh Jackman himself.

Hugh chuckled and said to me, "Hey, Jim, are you okay?" Stunned that he knew me—and by name!—I shared with him my apology for being so clumsy; the music director had requested my presence in his room.

Hugh diverted and thanked me for hiring so many of his friends from New York, as he has enjoyed his time together with them. I then shared with him that this was to be our last show together. At which, he responded, "Why? Am I going to die?" Now it was my turn to laugh.

"No, I certainly hope not, but this is the last of my performances for this tour." He assured me that our paths would cross again as he was planning future tours.

We were about to separate ways when I said, "You know, Mr. Jackman, we were told not to bother you." He listened attentively. "But at the risk of offending you...." Hugh jumped in, "Jim, I would love to have a selfie with my New York contractor." Without hesitation, I pointed my phone at the two of us and snapped a shot. Then, to my astonishment, he asked me to text him a copy; I was floored.

Jim and Hugh at The Prudential Center, Newark, New Jersey
—8 October 2019

HEARTACHE

"Hope is the power of being cheerful in
circumstances that we know to be desperate."
–G.K. Chesterton

On 17 September 1914, Francesco returned to Enna upon learning his father died. The death occurred just six weeks after the start of World War I. These two synchronous events would turn out to haunt Francesco for the remainder of his life.

Returning and ultimately staying in Sicily turned out to be his downfall. The people of Enna did not recognize his fame as a composer and conductor. What he had enjoyed in Germany did not translate to his fellow Sicilians. Sadly, as a result, he had no musical prospects. One small blessing was that he secured the post of deputy director of the Mother Church of Enna, directed by the aging Antonio Rizzo, and a position in the municipality of Enna.

In accepting the deputy director post, Neglia negotiated that only sacred music be performed in the chapel, as he wished to reinforce the sacred repertoire in religious worship. Unfortunately, his request was the cause of severe arguments, and soon great resistance began. The orchestral members became extremely rebellious, displaying their disdain during rehearsals. They purposely missed musical entrances and started talking while in rehearsals. Their actions caused Francesco to take disciplinary measures against those disrespecting him and his position.

Francesco turned to the Mother Church administrators for intervention but obtained little support. The dean of the cathedral, Dr. Mario Arengi, and the bishop of Piazza Armerina, Monsignor

Mario Sturzo, brother of the famous Don Luigi Sturzo, stood by his side, however. But, unfortunately, they didn't have any more influence over the insubordination than Francesco did. Tensions rose to an extraordinary level, so much so that on 3 March 1917, Francesco had to appear in front of the Caltanissetta Criminal Court to testify about an unfortunate event that took place months earlier, on 13 August 1916.

Francesco had conducted one of his own works during the solemn Mass. Of course, he wanted the performance to be well accepted by the musicians and the public. But some of the musicians purposely sabotaged his work, refusing to adjust to Francesco's baton. Despite his patience, the musicians resisted. The disruption rose to such a level that during the performance, laughter broke out in the orchestra. The laughter was loud enough for all performing and attending to see and hear.

In sheer frustration and blinded by anger, Francesco exclaimed, "You dare to laugh? Bestione [beast]!" Gaetano Contino, an amateur composer and violinist purposely made mistakes so that the piece of music itself would fail. This destruction of Francesco's music served as a severe provocation, and Francesco would not stand for it.

In an excerpt from the Court of Caltanissetta, the Dean of Castrogiovanni (Enna) Cathedral stated, "Offending those who offend is often the only way that the exasperated soul of the offended can find to protect oneself from the injury suffered."

Although Francesco was acquitted, the prosecution focused on Francesco being from Germany and, therefore, he must be a traitor. They insinuated that Francesco received subsidies from the German government via Switzerland, giving Francesco the nickname *spia Tedesco* or German spy.

The spy theory took root, and soon all of Francesco's correspondence was censored and delivered to Francesco by the Enna public security delegate. His wife and children were repeatedly insulted and even stoned while walking on the street. His financial situation was also worsening; his savings had run out, and his current salary was not nearly enough to support his family.

To rebuild his artistic life, he wanted to be transferred to Trieste to work as an elementary school teacher. A family friend, the Honorable Napoleone Colajanni, forwarded his transfer request to the Honorable Bernini, Minister of Public Education. But his recommendation fell on deaf ears. Bernini replied in a letter dated 9 January 1919, "He has a German wife and last year was harassed because of his family condition. Given this, I do not believe that, if new schools open in Trieste, he can be chosen as a teacher."

Francesco was not even given a chance to conduct a concert in any city in Italy. Further, all the conservatories rejected him as a teacher. Even the recommendations of Richard Strauss, Siegfried Wagner, Guglielmo Zuelli, Giacomo Puccini, Marco Enrico Bossi, and other highly esteemed musicians were of no use.

Francesco attempted to conduct a benefit concert in Bologna and applied to be the director of the musical high school but had no luck with either possibility. Shortly after that, he traveled to Rome, where he met Maestro Molinari. Molinari promised him to schedule a performance of his *Venetian Suite* at the Augusteo. Still, soon after the promise, a letter from Marco Enrico Bossi brought him the news that the performance would be impossible.

"Dear Master, I have had the opportunity to talk to Maestro Molinari on the subject that interests you. I have argued that for the moment (and that is for the next season), it is impossible to keep you in mind both as a conductor and as a composer. His reasons must be truly enormous if well-regarded Masters like you are to be neglected! Do not be discouraged by this and continue with faith in the tiring but luminous path of art.

With the sincerest esteem, and best regards to you.

Your dear Marco Enrico Bossi"

Letter from M.E. Bossi, Camerlata 12 July 1916
photo credit Mario Barbieri, *FP Neglia, La Vita Le Opera*

Since his father's passing, his daily struggles, sorrows, and bitterness continued. Despite all his problems, he continued to compose music. During this dark period, he wrote two Masses, a Major Compline, four Tantum Ergo, three Responsories for Holy Week, an Alma Pastorale, Litanies, songs, and the *Missa Brevis*.

The *Missa Brevis* was performed in France, Portugal, Germany, Japan, and many Italian cities. It was also performed several times in the Vatican and often on solemn occasions. Performances took place on 10 April 1962 at an Easter Mass, and again on 6 January 1964 for the feast day of the Epiphany. Both times were during the religious celebrations where the Pope offered the mass. Francesco's brother, my grandfather, Angelo, attended at least one of these performances.

One critic wrote about Francesco's *Missa Brevis*:

> The importance of this Mass lies in the musical language used, not the usual composition based on the resolution of harmonious basses. It is not a simple exercise in counterpoint but stems from Neglia's religious sentiment and outstanding ability as a musical craftsman. Neglia defined his being a musician as an apostolic service to art, and where it presented difficulties, he responded with humility. This Mass is forged by an artist's sensitivity, the technique of a craftsman, and his humankind's spirituality.

He continued:

> The tonal sequence that recalls the cello expresses a metaphysical singing that comes directly from the instruments, or rather from their soul. The cello, an instrument with a dark, rich timbre, is comparable to a low voice, a voice just like that of the singers chosen for this Mass. The use of dark and deep tones represents a search in the soul's depth, where the composer keeps hidden the inexpressibility that only in music can approach an ineffable saying. The whole Mass is transformed into a great allegory in which voices and organs become symbols of a profound spirituality from Neglia, the man, the artist, displaying all his brilliance in this work.

I find it remarkable that there are such reviews and critiques recognizing Francesco's greatness and talents, yet this period of his life was insufferable and extremely challenging.

To recover from his precarious position, he resumed his literary studies and obtained a degree as a German teacher from The University of Palermo. He moved to the small town of Caltanissetta in central Sicily in the autumn of 1919 to teach until 1921.

Teaching diploma obtained by Neglia at
the R. Conservatory of Palermo
photo credit Laura Fusaro, *Maestro sul podio e nella vita*

His stay in Caltanissetta was happy and serene, and Francesco was slowly regaining his confidence. In addition to being a teacher of the German language at the Technical Institute, he also gave private music lessons and organized symphonic concerts with the local Nissena Philharmonic. Additionally, he began to relive some of his past time in Hamburg as he was appointed music director at the provincial orphanage.

Francesco Paolo. in Vanzago, Italy with his students –1921
photo credit Mario Barbieri, *FP Neglia, La Vita Le Opera*

In Caltanissetta, he enjoyed a healthy salary, which allowed him to maintain his family's comforts with ease. The critical, most influential personalities in town held him in great esteem, and all liked him greatly. Although everything seemed to be falling into place, the city could not offer him the possibility of rebuilding the artistic life like the one he had laboriously built in Germany. Francesco truly missed that period and continued to aspire to reach those goals.

At forty-seven, he was too young to give up his dream as an artist, regardless of his high salary in Caltanissetta. He believed that to regain his German success, he would need to move to a larger city, Milan. In his earnest pursuit to gain back his musical life, he entered a teaching competition, for, if he won, he would have the possibility of moving to a larger city. As good fortune sometimes lends a hand, Francesco won first place.

Francesco learned that Milan was not one of the possible locations to relocate. He was offered three choices, Tola, Rome, or Vanzago. Due to its geographic location, just 25 kilometers from Milan, he chose Vanzago, and in 1921, he moved. He hoped that the proximity to Milan would help facilitate his musical recovery.

Unfortunately, while in Vanzago, Francesco's life once again began to spiral downward. His situation was precarious at best, so much so that the mayor offered to host him and his family in a large room in Town Hall. When a gentleman named Giussani learned that Francesco had moved into town but could not afford his own piano, he offered him the opportunity to play his piano for a few hours a day.

Although dejected, Francesco found the strength to compose and score the third act of his only opera, *Zelia,* although his dreams and vision of musical recovery were slipping away.

MARIA NEGLIA

"I have to earn every person in my life" –Maria Neglia

One of Francesco Paolo's brothers was my grandfather, Angelo. Angelo had two children, my father and my aunt Maria. Music is indeed in our bloodline and was very much alive in Maria. From her earliest days, she displayed controlled technique on the violin. Although her career didn't end until her retirement at 85 years, I am dedicating this chapter to her early years.

In one of the articles I found on Maria, the author explains her early days; it reads in part:

> Maria's father, Professor Angelo Neglia, was one of Italy's noted conductors and foremost violin teachers. At the age of 3½, Maria began lessons with her father, as her talent was already evident from that early age. She astounded her father by playing scales with ease and clarity, and by the age of five, she was already performing in some of Italy's larger concert halls.

My aunt's busy schedule had often prevented us from seeing each other on a regular basis. After I was thirteen, in 1976, our paths barely ever crossed again. But my memories are vivid, and my research has also proved to be fruitful.

In addition to my research, Maria sent me many documents and photographs marking important events in her life some years ago, as she was hoping to have a website constructed. I was helping her sort through all the items, which made her very happy. We were in the process of creating her website when she decided to retire. Just two short years after her retirement announcement, she passed away. Many of the possessions she sent me are shared in this book, and my hope is that by the time this book is published, I will have created the online presence she earned.

While preparing this chapter, I was fortunate enough to come across many of Maria's MCA (Music Corporation of America) announcements from the 1950s. Because I love the way many of them were crafted, I decided to share several of them in this chapter.

Press Relations Department MCA
598 Madison Avenue, New York

Maria Neglia, the fiery young violinist, owes her presence in the United States to an American Army sergeant.

Soon after the Americans began their occupation of Germany, Sargent Mike Spector walked into an entertainment hall of the army camp at Rosenheim, Germany. One of the attractions of the evening was a teenage violinist, an Italian girl named Maria Neglia.

As Maria started playing, Sargent Spector leaned forward attentively; a hush settled over the audience. A former theatrical agent, Spector knew good talent when he heard it. The enthusiastic cheers of the GI audience bore him out; this girl was good! After the performance, he got together with Maria and promised her that he would make every effort to get her into the United States upon returning to civilian life.

Mike Spector never forgot his promise, and in November 1948, he succeeded in booking her into the Park Avenue lounge in Miami. Overnight she became a sensation. From Miami, she moved into the Palmer House in Chicago, where she was such a hit that the management, for the first time in its history, booked her for an immediate return engagement.

Among other top spots, she played the Plaza in New York, the Radisson in Minneapolis, and Copley Plaza in Boston. On television, she appeared on Ed Sullivan's "Toast of the Town", Arthur Godfrey's "Talent Scouts", and on "Cavalcade of Bands."

It was a far cry from an army recreation center in Rosenheim, Germany, but if you ask Mike Spector, he will tell you she belonged there all the time.

After visiting a friend at CBS, where Spector watched entertainers such as Bing Crosby and Guy Lombardo rehearse, he decided to try his hand at managing artists.

Grandfather Angelo on the left, Maria in the center, and Senator George Smathers on the far right.

When World War II began, Spector went overseas with the U.S. 3rd Army in the 118th Signal Intelligence Company under General George S. Patton. After the war, he worked as a talent scout with Universal Pictures but got pink-slipped in the aftermath of a 1947 merger. That's when he moved to South Florida and decided to open a record store. The first Spec's debuted on Dixie Highway in Coral Gables in 1948.

In 1952 while in the United States, from Italy on a visitor's permit, Maria became a celebrity without even knowing it. Let me explain.

It started when Maria appeared on the Arthur Godfrey Television Show out of Miami. Florida's Senator George Smathers saw the show and was highly impressed with Maria's talent and warm personality. When he learned her permit was set to expire in the next few months, he introduced a bill to Congress which would allow her to remain in this country. As one of Maria's sponsors, Godfrey sent a glowing letter to

Washington on Maria's behalf, as did many others. My father Giuseppe is also mentioned in the bill. Upon moving to America, he used the English translation of his name, Joseph.

The document, which made it possible for my family to stay in the United States, is reproduced here:

FROM THE LAW LIBRARY
HOUSE OF REPRESENTATIVES

REPORT No. 614
83RD CONGRESS, 1ˢᵗ Session

MARIA NEGLIA AND ANGELO NEGLIA

18 JUNE 1953. Committed to the Committee of
the Whole House and ordered to be printed.
Mr. GRAHAM, from the Committee on the
Judiciary, submitted the following

REPORT
[To accompany S. 604]

The Committee on the Judiciary, to whom has referred the bill (S. 604) for the relief of Maria Neglia and Angelo Neglia, having considered the same, report favorably thereon without amendment and recommend that the bill do pass.

PURPOSE OF THE BILL

The purpose of the bill is to grant the status of permanent residence in the United States to Maria Neglia and Angelo Neglia. The bill provides for appropriate quota deductions and for the payment of the required visa fees.

GENERAL INFORMATION

The beneficiaries of the bill are father and daughter. They were born in Italy on 9 January 1896, and 7 August 1927, respectively, and last entered the United States as visitors on February 21, 1949. Miss Neglia is an accomplished violinist, and her father is presently acting as secretary and manager for her.

A letter, with the attached memorandum, dated 3 April 1953, to the chairman of the Senate Committee on the Judiciary from the Commissioner of Immigration and Naturalization with reference to the case reads as follows:

3 APRIL 1963.

Hon. WILLIAM LANGER,
Chairman, Committee on the Judiciary, United States Senate, Washington, D.C.

DEAR SENATOR: In response to your request of the Department of Justice for a report relative to the bill (S. 604) for the relief of Maria Neglia, Angelo Neglia, and Giuseppe Neglia, there is annexed a memorandum of information from the Immigration and Naturalization Service files concerning the beneficiaries.

According to the files of this Service, Giuseppe Neglia adjusted his immigration status in 1952 by departing to Canada and returning to the United States as a permanent resident. The bill would grant the other two aliens permanent residence in the United States upon payment of the required visa fees. It also would direct that the required quota numbers be deducted from the appropriate immigration quota.

Since the aliens are chargeable for the quota for Italy, which is oversubscribed, immigrant visas are not readily obtainable.

Sincerely,
-Commissioner.

MEMORANDUM OF INFORMATION FROM IMMIGRATION AND NATURALIZATION SERVICE Files RE: MARIA NEGLIA, ANGELO NEGLIA, AND GIUSEPPE NEGLIA, BENEFICIARIES OF S. 601.

Giuseppe Neglia, who has adjusted his immigration status, should not be included in the bill. The aliens, Angelo and Maria Neglia are father and daughter. They are natives and citizens of Italy who were born on 9 January 1896, and 7 August 1927, respectively. They last entered the United States on 21 February 1949, in Miami, Florida, as visitors for two months. The period of their temporary stay was subsequently extended to 20 August 1949. They had originally entered this country on 18 October 1948, at the port of New York as visitors for a period of 6 months and thereafter departed on 6 February 1949.

On 10 May 1949, H. R. 4630 was introduced in the 81st Congress on the aliens' behalf but was not enacted. On 10 January 1952, S. 2386 was introduced in the 82nd Congress on their behalf and was not enacted. Warrants for their arrest in deportation proceedings were issued on 9 April 1952, charging that they were immigrants not in possession of valid immigration visas at the time of their entry. At the hearings accorded them under the warrants of arrest, they were granted the privilege of departing from the United States voluntarily in lieu of deportation. The aliens, Angelo and Maria Neglia failed to depart. On 5 February 1953, a stay of deportation was directed in their cases pending consideration of the instant bill.

Miss Neglia is a violinist by profession. Her average weekly income is about $500.00. Mr. Angelo Neglia is presently acting as secretary and manager for his daughter, for which he receives $60 to $70 a week. The aliens have no dependents in the United States. Their only relative residing in this country is Giuseppe Neglia, who is the brother of Maria Neglia.

Senator George Smathers, the author of the bill, has written to the chairman of the Senate Judiciary Committee as follows:

UNITED STATES SENATE, COMMITTEE ON INTERIOR AND INSULAR AFFAIRS

27 February 1968.

Honorable WILLIAM E. LANGER,
Chairman, Senate Judiciary Committee,
United States Senate, Washington, D. C.

DEAR SENATOR: S. 604, an immigration bill for the relief of Maria Neglia, et al., introduced by me, has been referred to your committee and your Immigration Subcommittee, I am informed. I am enclosing herewith a brief covering the history, activities, and other information of interest in connection with this family, for the advice and consideration of the subcommittee handling this legislation.

Let me say that this is one bill on which I am very hopeful early action will be taken. I shall therefore appreciate anything which you and your committee may be able to do to have consideration of it expedited.

Thanking you and with kindest regards,

Sincerely yours,
GEORGE SMATHERS, United States Senator

The history of the beneficiaries of the bill is contained in the following statement:

HISTORY OF ANGELO NEGLIA AND MARIA NEGLIA

Angelo Neglia, age 67, was born on 9 January 1886, in Enna, Sicily, Italy, of a musical family, the son of Giuseppe and Maria (née Greca) Neglia. His father's occupation was that of the local orchestra conductor, who also taught music in his community.

After graduating from the local high school at the age of 17, Angelo volunteered for service in the Italian Army in the Music Corps. It was during these days that he furthered his music studies which had been started under his father.

From 1915 to 1918, Mr. Neglia was called back into service during the First World War and was a sergeant in the Italian Army affiliated with the Allied Governments. He was honorably discharged from the army, after which he continued studying and began to conduct various orchestras and lead various bands throughout the entire Italian peninsula. At the age of 34, in the year 1920, he established a music school at Reggio Calabria. At this point, Mr. Neglia began his training school of music for children, following which he became quite well known throughout Italy, and his services were in great demand.

In 1926, at the age of 40, Mr. Neglia established another school at Trieste, Italy. It was here that Maria and Giuseppe Neglia were born to him and Maria's mother, Dora. Maria was born in 1927, and Giuseppe was born in 1929. Having established this fine music training school for children, it followed that Mr. Neglia would teach his daughter music. For the following five years, from 1927 to 1932, Angelo trained his daughter, Maria, for violin and found her to be a child prodigy, whereupon the Neglia family began to travel on concert tours, Maria giving her first concert at the age of 5.

From 1932 to 1938, this family traveled all over Italy, and Mr. Neglia kept training his child, teaching her and arranging her concert career.

It was during the year 1938, after Maria's brother, Giuseppe, had been placed in a private school in Bologna, Italy, remaining there until 1941, that Mr. Neglia took his family to Berlin, and here Maria gave a concert at the Winter Garden for 1 month's engagement. As a result of this engagement, this child's violin artistry was recognized. Many contracts were negotiated for Maria for a period of 1 year all over Germany, followed by engagements in Czechoslovakia, Poland, Denmark, Austria, Luxembourg, and Strasbourg.

Private tutors handled Maria's schooling, and her mother and father managed to teach her whenever it was impossible to get private instruction.

From 1938 to 1941, when Europe became engulfed in the Second World War, the Neglia family would constantly leave every country that was engaged in war and would take concert engagements only where they were able to escape military entanglements, playing for neutral zones wherever possible.

From 1941 to 1945, during the time of the Second World War, when the United States took part in this world fiasco, the Neglia's spent most of their time in Austria, constantly avoiding the bombed cities and war fronts. It was here that they were in constant fear of getting into political entanglements and further found themselves in great fear of the Nazis, Communists, and the Fascists. At this time, they realized how Italian boys were being lured to Germany with promises of work only to find themselves without food and very few opportunities to earn a living. They could see at this point the fraud that was being perpetrated upon the Italian people and the fear that was encompassing all free people. They could constantly see around them the penalty of speaking their piece. They dared not express their sentiments or opinions regarding the political situation. They found themselves traveling from city to city, losing all their personal belongings, going into underground shelters and constantly avoiding bombings and capable of trusting no one for fear of prosecution. Further, they were in daily anticipation of corporal punishment and arrest because of the numerous spies who were always around them attempting to pry information from them since they had been traveling.

The small threesome continued to move eastward toward the free countries, looking for a possible engagement where they could be paid a living wage or at least breathe free air once again. Finally, in 1945, while fleeing from the Russians, they were forced to leave everything they owned, lost all their money, and, in an attempt to get transportation from one city to another, they slept on cattle trains, took any conveyance possible, and found themselves in Germany, 2 miles from Austria, where the city was overtaken by the Americans.

Here, Maria and her father asked the American officers if they could entertain the soldiers. After being investigated and finding that they were free of all political entanglements, they were allowed to entertain the American soldiers in camps and hospitals or wherever groups gathered. At this time, Maria's father, Angelo Neglia, met an American sergeant by the name of Martin W. Spector, who had been a talent scout and an artist's agent in America. It was Mr. Spector who recognized Maria's talent and stated that he would get Maria to the United States and have her play her violin for American audiences at some future date. This young lady played for the American forces during this time, giving 70 percent of her work as charity recitals. Her father took whatever engagements were offered, and played for special services of the Armed Forces and continued to work for the Red Cross, hospitals, mess halls, officers' clubs without pay the majority of the time and, whenever possible, took engagements that would reimburse them for their time and effort.

The Neglia family returned to Italy in March 1948 and received a communication from Mr. Spector, who negotiated a contract with the Neglia's to have them come to the United States, whereupon he would supply their visitor's visas and the necessary funds in return for a 5-year contract. He became her personal manager for a consideration of 25 percent of all the fees she received while playing here in the United States. Angelo, abandoning everything he had in Italy in order to allow Maria this opportunity, came to America with Maria and Giuseppe, and the mother remained in Italy with relatives. It was necessary for the father to come over as Maria's manager and director, while her brother, who had studied English, came as an interpreter and was able to help them orientate themselves in this country.

Maria's first engagement in the United States was at the Park Avenue Lounge in Miami Beach, Florida. Following this engagement, she entered into a contract with the Music Corporation of America. Approximately one year later, she accepted special engagements wherever she was sent throughout the United States. Presently, Miss Neglia is engaged at the Vagabond Club in Miami, Florida, and has had a very successful run, having been singled out by Mr. Arthur Godfrey for his television show originating in New York.

Maria and her father are presently residing in Miami, Florida, and her brother is married to an American citizen in the city of New York. Her contract with Mr. Spector runs out in May of this year.

The Music Corporation of America has offered her a renewal contract, and several other offers have been forthcoming, which are pending executions upon determination of her residency status.

Angelo Neglia and Maria Neglia have shown their great love for this country by doing a tremendous amount of charitable work, the evidence of which is attached to this brochure. They have saved some of their money, been prudent and industrious in their attempt to adjust themselves to this new life, and Maria has found herself capable of speaking the English language with much fluidity and, in her own words, loves the American type of life. Her ability to imitate the youth of America is shown in being interested in our schools, our Government, our American culture, and advances in radio and television. All of this is evident in her charitable performances throughout the country.

In addition to the above, Senator Smathers has submitted numerous letters and recommendations on behalf of the beneficiaries of the bill, referring to the outstanding talent of Mr. and Miss Neglia and the numerous charitable performances which she has given on behalf of various meritorious groups.

After consideration of all the facts in the case, the committee is of the opinion that the bill (S. 604) should be enacted.

Angelo, with his daughter, Maria

Here are some of the recommendation letters that were sent to Senator Smathers on the family's behalf.

E. L. COTTON, Inc.
REAL ESTATE
SPECIALIZING IN
COUNTRY ESTATES, GROVES
ACREAGE AND FARMLANDS

5830 SOUTH DIXIE HIGHWAY
PHONE 87-5371

101 N. STATE HIGHWAY
SOUTH MIAMI 43, FLORIDA

February 17, 1953

Senator George A. Smathers
U. S. Congress
Washington, D. C.

Dear Sir:

Our attention has been directed to the application of Miss Maria Neglia and her father, Angelo Neglia, for permanent residency in the United States.

We have been acquainted with Miss Neglia and her father for about three years, and have been favorably impressed.

We have advised Mr. Neglia as to several real estate investments in this area, some of which are income-producing, and others which are merely buy and sell investments. He has expressed his intention to so invest if he receives authority for permanent residency.

Everything, personally or relating to business matters, seems to indicate that they are of the solid-citizen type, i. e., that they keep an eye to the future by thriftiness and wise investments, and that they are consequently appreciative of the best course to pursue in financial matters.

Thus, indications are that their future, if granted permanent residency, would be financially secure.

Our highest regards.

Very truly yours,
E. L. COTTON, INC.

By *E. L. Cotton*
E. L. Cotton

C:gh

VON ARX AND VON ARX
ATTORNEYS AT LAW
502 BISCAYNE BUILDING
19 W. FLAGLER STREET
MIAMI, FLORIDA

JOSEPH A. VON ARX
LUCILLE M. VON ARX
TELEPHONE 2-1726

February 7, 1953

Honorable George Smathers,
United States Senator,
Senate Building,
Washington, D. C.

Dear Senator Smathers:

I have represented Miss Maria Neglia and her father, Angelo Neglia, for over a period of one year in various legal matters which have disclosed their financial position and I have found them to be completely independent of any state aid or other charitable needs.

Miss Neglia has had an average salary of over four hundred dollars ($400.00) a week and has been able to live well within her means and, in turn, her father, who has managed her affairs as well as directing her, has constantly insisted upon partial savings above and beyond their expenses in order to assure themselves that in the event she was not engaged in her profession she would have enough money to tide her over any emergency period.

Further, Miss Neglia has provided herself with accident insurance in the event anything should happen to her earning power. Presently, Mr. Neglia and his daughter are negotiating for several types of indemnity insurance policies. May I further add that Miss Neglia and her father are extremely industrious people and have indicated that they are not foolish or irresponsible in their business matters and seem to show good judgment in all decisions that require the negotiation of contracts and the disbursement of moneys received.

I cannot state enough complimentary phrases covering the conduct of the said people. They are extremely well educated, and show good breeding. They have all the attributes of excellent citizens and I most heartily recommend any assistance that can be given to these people to allow them to become permanent residents of The United States.

Very truly yours,

Lucille M. Von Arx

LUCILLE M. VON ARX

LMVA:hb

COMMAND AND GENERAL STAFF COLLEGE

Fort Leavenworth, Kansas

22 B Stilwell Avenue
19 January 1953

TO: The Honorable Members of the Eighty-Third Congress.

It is a sincere pleasure for me to recommend to you Professor Angelo NEGLIA and his daughter, Maria NEGLIA, to be permitted to remain in the United States under a permanent Visa by a Special Bill before Congress.

I have known the NEGLIAs since 1946 when I was the director of the United States Army Special Services Civilian Show Circuit. I was under the command of Major General A. R. Boling, Chief of Special Services, European Command, and directed the Show Circuit from a headquarters in Heidelberg, Germany. In this capacity, I contracted for the services of Miss NEGLIA as a solo violinist and her father as her accompanist, teacher, and manager. Miss NEGLIA and her father entertained our soldiers throughout the American Zone of Germany, assisting materially in maintaining their morale, and were considered our finest and most appreciated artists. In addition, my personal impression of the NEGLIAs was one of respect for their excellent character and perfect behavior. There was only praise for them from the various subordinate Special Services Officers, particularly for their commendable personal traits.

I met the NEGLIAs again in July 1952 in Miami, Florida, and found that they had not changed from the kind, lovable people I knew them for in Europe. They seem to have adapted themselves perfectly to our American Way of Life. and, in my humble opinion, would make excellent citizens of our country.

If there is any way by which I can vouch for them more officially, I would be happy to do so.

Subscribed before me this
19th day of January, 1953.

Respectfully,

CLAUDE L. PRIDGEN
Lieutenant Colonel, U. S. Army
0-38965

Maria's first knowledge that President Eisenhower had signed the bill came via a long-distance phone call from Godfrey in New York. His opening words were reported to be, "Congratulations, You're in! Be sure to go to the immigration office and get your green card!"

Maria burst into grateful tears, the happiest she had ever shed. In 1958 Maria became a citizen of the United States. The United States also welcomed her as an artist so sought after that she was booked 52 weeks a year at all the top nightclubs, concert halls, and television programs.

During World War II, and after she had appeared in virtually every major city in Europe, Maria volunteered to work for the U. S.

Army Special Services. She was a front-line entertainer for Allied troops throughout the Continent, and many of the G.I.s, fondly remember her as "the tiny fiddler with the expressive eyes."

Arthur Godfrey insisted that Maria share with their television audience Maria's favorite and most beautiful words she knows: the preamble to the United States Constitution! She shared that the three greatest thrills for her life were the first time she saw the Statue of Liberty; the news that a special bill had been passed by Congress allowing her to stay in America; and performing at the White House for President Eisenhower.

Maria played before President Eisenhower on three different occasions. On the first occasion, she walked up to the President and said: "I had to thank you in person for making it possible for me to stay here." As a result, the President was so touched that he devoted a 10-minute speech before the 700 people assembled on immigration and the bills he had to sign each day.

Arthur Godfrey "Wednesday TV Show"

He described how he felt when a talented young lady came to him and thanked him in person, bringing home firmly the realization of how many human beings were affected by the printed pages to which he attached his signature. Maria broke into tears, tears of happiness and amazement that the United States President could be talking about her.

Another time, Maria received a wire from Mrs. Eisenhower, asking her to appear at a party in the White House. When the news came, without hesitation, she booked a flight from Las Vegas, where she was engaged, to the White House. The third time, Maria was invited to appear at the Alfalfa Dinner, where the President was also a guest. She flew up from Miami this time commenting, "No distance is too great for me to cover in order to play for the President."

President Eisenhower inscribed the photograph "For Maria
Neglia with best wishes to an accomplished artist."
(*left to right*): Joey Bishop, unidentified, Steve Allen, President
Eisenhower, Eileen Barton(?), unidentified, Eddie Fisher, and Maria.

Shortly after her entry and first series of performances in the United States, reporters wrote about her very favorably.

Press Relations Department, MCA
598 Madison Avenue New York 22, New York

The vivacious virtuoso of the violin made her American debut as a teenager at Miami Beach's Park Avenue Lounge and won immediate acclaim for her prowess as both a masterful instrumentalist and subtle pantomimist.

The sleek and chick Maria possesses a devastating sense of humor that is at once apparent when she performs. Offstage, her humorous asides have proven to be miniature blockbusters. President Dwight D. Eisenhower, Florida's Senator George Smathers, and fellow-show business stars that include Bob Hope, Arthur Godfrey, Jackie Gleason, Martha Raye, Kate Smith, Jack Paar, and Ed Sullivan, among the many, can attest to her talents as a delightfully warm human being, one who is as serious about her music and the violin as she is sensible in going through life loving people and enjoying life to the fullest extent possible.

In an age when the musical masters, Heifetz and Kreisler, are considered geniuses, Maria Neglia, the foremost classical and pop player of her sex, has been dubbed 'the petite, brunette female Columbus who has made Americans discover how exciting and entertaining a violin can be!'

Maria appeared as the headliner of many Nightclubs throughout the United States, including New York's Plaza Hotel and Copacabana, Pittsburgh's Holiday House, Chicago's Palmer House and Chez Paree Chicago, the Biltmore Bowl in Los Angeles, Ciro's in Hollywood, Sahara in Las Vegas, Riverside in Reno, Vagabonds Club in Miami, Miami Beach's Fontainebleau and the Americana, San Juan International in

San Juan, Puerto Rico, the Town Casino in Buffalo, Henry Grady in Atlanta, Chase Club in St. Louis, The National in Havana, Cuba, and the Roosevelt in New Orleans.

Maria's New York concert performances included Carnegie Hall, Town Hall, Radio City Music Hall, The Roxy Theatre, and The Palace Theatre. In Chicago, she performed at the famed Chicago Theatre.

She kept journals where she recorded an accurate snapshot, in writing, of the day's events. When I came upon them, I was taken aback. Seeing Maria's journals made me pause to reflect. Not only were we connected through music, but now I learned that we enjoy documenting our lives just as Peppino did.

Maria collected many quotes from newspaper articles and other reviews. They include: "The violin is the most beautiful instrument there is, and I refuse to believe that anyone doesn't like it." and "You don't play the violin with just your fingers or a wind instrument with just your lips. You play with your whole self." "I didn't learn how to play the violin; it was born in me." "Playing the violin is not my job or hobby; it is a way of life."

Regarding her dozens of television performances, she commented that "more people than ever before in history are being exposed to great music. Even those who listen to popular music will upgrade themselves. There are 14 million high-fidelity sets in the country, and I believe that television awakened the interest of most of them to good music."

I spoke to my half-sister, Dina, who knew our father better than I did. During our exchange, she shared that back in 2000 or 2001, she, along with her brothers, played a chamber music concert in the home of Mike Spector in Florida.

Martin "Mike" Spector was the owner of Spec's Music stores in Florida. Dina shared that our father and Mike had a very warm relationship and that our father spoke fondly of Mike. I later learned that Mike died in 2003 at age 98 and that he has living children—Ann,

Mike, and Rosalind—who are probably in their 60s. Dina thought that they might be able to shine a bit more light on Maria and her career.

I googled Ann Spector and discovered her website. After reading up on her, it became evident that the acorn did not fall far from the tree. Like her father, she was in the music business. Over the years, her responsibilities expanded as she moved up the ranks at Spec's Music to store manager, buyer, merchandiser, president, and ultimately Chief Executive Officer.

In 1985, Ann was integral in taking the family business public, and its stock was traded on NASDAQ under the symbol SPEK. After going public, the company expanded to over 80 stores in Florida and Puerto Rico. In 1998 the company merged with Camelot Music. Soon after, Camelot merged with Transworld Entertainment making Spec's part of a 1,000-store chain at the time.

Spec's Record shop, Miami, Florida

I am sorry that I never had the opportunity to meet with Mike himself, as he was single-handedly responsible for opening the door to my family immigrating to the United States.

In January 2021, I picked up the phone and dialed Ann. The opening to our conversation was a bit awkward, not because of anything she said, but more due to my tentative opening. It went something like this, "Hello; I would like to speak to Ann" She responded with, "this is Ann." Tongue-tied, I continued with "you don't know me, but I am calling about your father, Mike, and his relationship with my aunt, Maria." There was silence on the other side of the phone, and for a good reason. I cleared my throat and continued, "I understand Mike was responsible for bringing my aunt to the United States."

Ann then took a breath and said, "Who is this, exactly, that I am speaking with?" "I'm Jim Neglia, nephew of Maria." And she added, "And the son of Joseph?" I chuckled but continued with, "Yes, he was my father."

Once the ice was broken, and we shared a good thirty-minute conversation, I told her I would follow up with an email, sharing with her my contact information. She had shared with me that at the time of her father's passing, she came in possession of most of his personal belongings, paperwork, photographs, and memorabilia from days gone by. She also shared that her father, up until the time of his death, had a photograph of Maria on his wall. Her voice lowered when she shared that "dad" never got over not being able to push Maria to the ultimate level of recognition. It was something he always regretted.

Ann had just finished getting her second cataract operation but added how efficient she was, regardless, and that she would begin to sift through the boxes and share her findings.

Angelo, Joseph, Maria, and Spector in Miami

Maria departing for a tour, and Spector seeing her off

Press Relations Department MCA
598 Madison Avenue, New York

MARIA NEGLIA PALMER HOUSE

That Maria has lived up to everything indicated in these first reviews can be seen from the record she's made since her first triumph. Immediately after her Miami debut, Maria was booked into one of the top show places of the nation, the Palmer House in Chicago. She made such a terrific hit there that they signed an act for an immediate return engagement for the first time in the Palmer House history. She closed in the middle of one month and reopened in the middle of the next.

From the Palmer House, she went on to play such spots as the Radisson Hotel in Minneapolis, the Olympia Theatre in Miami, the Plaza Hotel in New York, the Copley Plaza in Boston, the Capitol Theatre in New York, the Chase Club in St. Louis and the Henry Grady in Atlanta winning the applause of audiences and the admiration of critics everywhere.

What is it about Maria Neglia that has brought her to the front rank of American entertainers in so short a time? Besides the fact that she is a first-rate violinist, the biggest factor in her meteoric rise to popularity is her brilliant showmanship.

When Maria plays, every facet of her personality is thrown into her performance—her facial expressions, body movement, and gestures all blend into the music and keep the audience entranced by the magic of the effect. The semi-classical and popular selections that make up her repertoire...lend themselves readily to her showmanship and technical skill. Maria Neglia is the epitome of good entertainment.

During my research, I was fortunate to come upon a series of reviews, press excerpts, or printed recognitions of Maria and her talents.

"If her first-night audience had its way, Maria Neglia would have still been playing. Europe doesn't have much that I thought this country wanted, but to get a bundle in reverse, when this bundle is the talented Maria, is wonderful."

–Paul Bruun in Miami Beach Florida Sun;
21 November 1948

"If Maria Neglia and her violin aren't the toast of the better establishments and musical soirees...yes, and of television before she's been in this country a year, then we will have lost faith in the taste of the public, the astuteness of show business, and the kindliness of those gods of fortune whose chore it is to see that worthy talent gets a just reward."

–George Bourke in Miami Herald; 23 November 1948

"The other night, I dropped in at Wingy Grober and Charlie Block's Park Avenue. It looked like mid-season, with Walter Winchell, Ed Sullivan, Ted Baker, Jack Friedlandre, Emil Schwartzhaupt, Ben Gaines, and other prominent folks in the audience. They rocked the joint with applause for Charlie Farrell, Luis Torres, the tremendous baritone, Maria Neglia, whose performance is something out of this world, and Peter Rich."

–Jack Kofoed in Miami Herald; 6 December 1948

"Be sure and catch an import named Maria Neglia at Wingy's Park Avenue. Rated one of the finest entertainers."

–Walter Winchell in Miami Herald; 27 November 1948

"Maria's talent is comparable to that of the most famous violinists of all time, including Kreisler, Heifetz, and many others."

–Dick Lowe in Miami Daily News; 23 November 1948

"For the column's Preferred List: The Brilliant artistry of pretty, 19-year-old Maria Neglia."

–Danton Walker in New York Daily News; 25 October 1949

"Maria Neglia, the Parisian Room star, is the nicest thing that's happened to a violin since Stradivarius."

–Frank Farrell in New York World-Telegram;
24 October 1949

"Miss Neglia, a 19-year-old Italian girl who's much prettier than Fritz Kreisler and most other violinists, can coax either moonlight or fireworks out of a fiddle, and she adds up to a wonderful earful all around."

–Bob Goddard in St. Louis Globe-Democrat;
26 February 1950

Maria performs on the "Toast of the Town" hosted by Ed
Sullivan at the Maxine Elliott Theater in New York City.
–1 August 1954
Photo credit, Steve Oroz/Michael Ochs

I was taken aback to read in the MCA notes on Maria's appearance
on the Joey Bishop Show that the announcer for the show was none
other than Regis Philbin. I am reminded of how many celebrities, and
personalities my aunt either knew, or met, during her career.

The Joey Bishop Show
Television Announcer: Regis Philbin

MARIA NEGLIA
28 October 1960- Taping
29 October 1960- Airing

TALKING POINTS:

My next guest started playing the violin at the age of 3½, turned professional at 5, and has played everywhere from the great concert halls of Europe to the White House. A big welcome for Maria Neglia!

She will perform "Zorba's Dance" from *Zorba the Greek* and "More." The orchestra will accompany both selections.

TALKING TOPICS:
Maria will recall her first meeting at the White House and performance for Dwight Eisenhower.

A special bill was passed in Congress granting her American citizenship. Senator Smathers of Florida saw her on The Arthur Godrey show and posed the bill. Maria claims she was "born in a valise with a violin in her hand." She appears tonight with a new gown, new material, but a 300-year-old violin.

Maria will show Joey her first violin and play "Little Spanish Flea" on it with the orchestra while sitting at the panel. This will be performed on the same instrument she played when she was 3½.

Maria was playing in Vienna when the Russians entered. She fled with her family and hitchhiked to the border. However, the ride with a truck driver nearly proved fatal. She and her brother, Joseph, were sitting in the back of the truck on a wooden crate when planes attacked but missed the truck. Later she found out the crate contained explosives.

Maria Neglia had undoubtedly had a very remarkable career. The honors and acclaim she has already received for her brilliant nightclub performances seem to be just a prelude to even greater ones ahead. Whether playing her violin on the concert stage or pitching Yuban Coffee in television commercials, Maria Neglia has the kind of personality and talent that makes you stop and take notice.

As soon as she walks on stage, audiences feel they know her, and they probably do! She has been featured on every top talk show, from The Tonight Show with Johnny Carson to "Merv." The video appearance that she is most proud of is her fantastic run of twenty-four (yes - 24) appearances on the great Ed Sullivan Show.

Ed Sullivan and Maria –27 August 1961

Press Relations Department MCA
598 Madison Avenue, New York

Where did this fine career begin? To answer that, we
have to journey back to her native home of Italy. At
the age of just five years old, Maria stood on stage for
the first time playing a specially constructed "baby"
violin. She received her first ovation before she quite
understood what all the cheering was about! But the
ovations and cheering continued as she launched a
unique career that made her familiar on concert stages,
nightclubs, and theatres across Europe.

Maria immigrated to the United States with her family.
Maria's star seemed to rise as soon as she first set foot in
America. In time she became an American citizen and
started a two-way love affair with American audiences,

enthralling audiences with her dynamic personality and stage presence.

Ms. Neglia has diversified her many talents to include acting, singing, and writing. Her recent commercials have introduced Maria to a whole new audience, who may be entirely unaware of her musical genius.

Maria Neglia is an artist who, bow in hand, shoots her way right into the hearts of her audience - without using a single arrow. She uses her violin instead.

Red Buttons cutting his birthday cake, Maria is just to his right

DIVERTISEMENTS

Frank Sinatra

MARIA NEGLIA
And Her Magic Violin

Music By
Sacasas and his Latin Orchestra
Jack Stuart Orchestra

Maria worked with Frank Sinatra on many occasions.

A compilation of photographs of Maria from
the age of two through her teen years.

I am happy to include all this material on Maria—a fascinating
period that displays the first part of her fantastic career. I hope you
enjoy these articles, news clippings, and photographs as much as I have
enjoyed writing about them.

"Italian child prodigy conducts the orchestra at eight years of age. Maria Neglia, daughter of a well-known music teacher, Maestro Angelo Neglia of Trieste, has startled Italy with the brilliance of violin playing and her skill as a conductor. Maria played at the Colonna Gallery, Rome, Italy, before a distinguished audience. –27 August 1937"

With Milton Berle

With Julius LaRosa

Jock Leydeh from the Daily News created this caricature of Maria

Fred Astaire inscribed a photograph, "To Maria
Neglia, Sincerely, Fred Astaire 1962"

Bob Hope inscribed, "To Maria Neglia,
Thanks for the Memory, Bob Hope."

With Peter Lawford

Bob and Mary Ann Fosse
Bob signs, "to Maria, you are a great artist, showman, and person.
Happiness and success will always be with you. Fondly, Bob 7/10/49"
From Mary Ann, "To Maria, A wonderful girl and a great artist.
We loved working with you and hope we will be together again real
soon. Bob and Mary Ann Fosse, Palmer House, Chicago, Il 49"

Steve Lawrence inscribed, "Dear Maria It is always a pleasure to work with you and an equal pleasure just to see you. Love Steve"

Pat Boone inscribed, "Maria Encore! Encore! Till our next tour - Warmest wishes, Pat."

Behind the scenes at CBS

On the set of Mike Douglas

Maria at 5

Maria with her first violin

Maria billed with Frank Sinatra

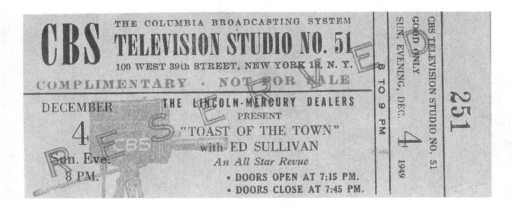

CBS Television Studio No. 51 Ticket
"Toast of the Town" with Ed Sullivan –4 December 1949

At the White House with President Richard Nixon
who inscribed a note "To Maria, with congratulations
to a fine artist -From Richard Nixon."

Specs Family Home, in Miami –circa 1955
Maria is on the floor while her father Angelo is seated in the back

CBS-TV Sparks Nugget

The Evening Post's cartoonist, Tony Grogan, was at the opening
night of the Kathy Kirby Show in the Showground Hall this week,
and this is how he saw the top-of-the-bill star and her supporting
cast: accompanist Don Phillips, rock singer Jess Conrad, comic
violinist Maria Neglia, folk-singer Nick Taylor, and compere Bob
Andrews. The show, which has been very well received, ends its
Port Elizabeth run tonight and then goes to East London.

Five-foot nothing of "sparkle with a violin" is Maria Neglia, who is In Town this week with the Kathy Kirby show. It starts at the Durban City Hall tonight at 8.15.

Italian by birth, American resident since a special law was passed in the United States to allow her to stay there, she comes from generations of serious musicians, went on the stage at the age of five.

Maria can make a violin talk. She can also make her audience laugh without saying a word. She has been called "the female Victor Borge," prefers to think of herself as "Just me!"

She has an apartment in New York, three poodles, loves driving, photography and animals, and her speciality in the cooking line is macaroni sauce and veal cutlets.

Her violin, made in 1681, is an Amati, insured for 10,000 dollars. Her hands are insured for 50,000 dollars.

["Mercury" photograph.

"Italian by birth, American resident since a special law was passed in the United State to allow her to stay there, she comes from generations of serious musicians, and went on stage at the age of five….She has been called 'the female Victor Borge,' prefers to think of herself as 'Just me!'…Her violin made in 1681 is an Amati, insured for 10,000 dollars, while her hands are insured for 50,000 dollars."

Maria performing live to a sold-out audience

"For Maria Neglia. With admiration for your marvelous artistry and my warmest personal regards, Always, Linda Darnell 1948"

Catrina Valente, Italian-French multilingual
singer, guitarist, dancer, and actress

Icedrome   Jerry Lewis

The Mike Douglas Show, starring Maria Neglia

Pat Boone

On the NBC Tonight Show with Johnny Carson
–Monday, 19 July 1971

Promo

OPENING TONIGHT!

MARIA NEGLIA

in Cabaret

in the

CAUSERIE

Couvert charge R1.00 per person

Please telephone 26681 for all table reservations

THE EDWARD

South Africa's Premier Hotel

Opening at the Causerie in South Africa

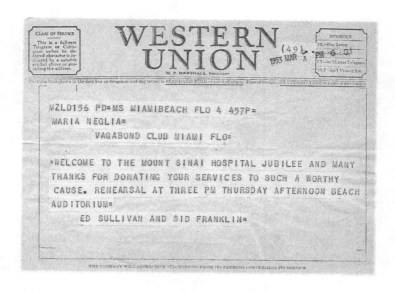

Western Union note from Ed Sullivan and Sid Franklin

SHANE

"A writer is a person for whom writing is more difficult
than it is for other people." –Leonard Bernstein

Shane is the son of a childhood friend, a friend who, for nearly my entire life, I have always considered family. Our families had grown up together, played together, went to school, worshiped together, and remained to this day just a phone call away.

Recently, Shane, his father Jimmy, and I met up one night in New York at Madison Square Garden before a Who show. It was a fantastic reunion for Jimmy and me, but to make it even more special, this was the first time I met Shane.

Like his father, Shane was a nice, caring, respectful young man, and our relationship took root. Sometime later, Shane was working on a project for school and asked for my assistance. A few months later, he shared with me the questions needed for his project.

1. When did you start learning music? Which instruments did you play, and what was your favorite?

I grew up in not only a musical family but a heritage of musicians that runs generations deep. I speak of my great uncle in-depth in my second book, *Center Stage*. With that in mind, my earliest memory of playing an instrument is when I was about four. This is when my father sat me down behind the piano and explained how to understand music in the most basic form. He shared what an interval is, what chords are, what the melody is, and what accompaniment is. After a few years behind the piano and having shown some proficiency, my parents thought it might be time to add another instrument to the piano.

When I was about six, my aunt Maria began teaching me to play the violin. I took lessons for a few years, on and off, due to her busy performance schedule. Although I liked the violin, I never really had the desire to make it as a violinist. Shortly after that, believe it or not, I picked up the trombone. One big reason to try the trombone was that my older brother (John) took up the trumpet, so it seemed natural for me to pick up a brass instrument. That chapter was short-lived.

Then, in the winter of 1975, when I was 12, my parents gave me a pair of drumsticks and a practice pad for Christmas. From day one, I was hooked and knew, without a doubt, I had found my true calling. Shortly after, I began lessons with Carl Wolf in Bloomfield, New Jersey ($7.00 per half hour). I displayed rapid acceleration with my daily exercises.

I kept up with my piano skills but dropped the violin and trombone. By the time I was 15, I had added the classical guitar to my daily practice routine. I still love playing the guitar, but as a young man, I adored drumming and worked incredibly hard at being the best drummer I could be.

In short, the drums were my love, but I cherish all the instruments that pushed me toward being a complete musician.

2. Who were your musical mentors/teachers? And if so, how did they push you towards your attitude to music?

My musical mentors began with my father, as he was responsible for introducing me to music. Years later, Carl Wolf, my first drum teacher, was an extremely serious character who pushed me very hard to practice and learn every week. But it wasn't until I was preparing for college that my true mentor entered my life. He was a caring, nurturing being named Ed Fay. Ed was a percussion teacher at William Paterson College, and it was he who prepared me for my college auditions and the start of my freelance career. I share much of this story in my first book, *Onward and Upward*.

Ed shared with me many of his philosophies and approaches to music, and more specifically, the approach of how to express myself on my instruments. Ed pushed me very hard to be a timpanist, as well as a soloistic snare drummer. He felt that if I could master those two instruments, I would have an excellent chance to succeed and find work as a percussionist and timpanist.

He guided me on the snare drum (14 inches in diameter), which would produce a very tight, intense sound versus the timpani, which could be as large as 32 inches in diameter, thus producing a lower, more tonal note. He felt that I would have the tools for an excellent chance to succeed if I could control the two extreme membrane instruments.

Ed was my musical hero until I auditioned at the three New York conservatories: The Juilliard School, The Manhattan College of Music, and The Mannes College of Music. I was accepted into all three, but Mannes offered me a scholarship and, ultimately, work studies assistance. Work studies came in the form of the position of librarian of the orchestra, a job that proved to be invaluable during my path forward as a newbie in the field.

While at Mannes, the demands that were thrust upon me were unparalleled; I had never experienced such a feeling of complete and utter immersion. Plain and simply put, Mannes kicked my backside daily. This was all led by my private percussion instructor, Walter Rosenberger. Walter (retired principal percussionist of the New York Philharmonic) altered my thinking as a musician more than any other teacher up until then. Walter would hold my hand, shape it around a stick or mallet, and marry me to his practical approach. To this day, when I hit a drum or play the tambourine, I can feel Walter pat me on my back as if he can hear and see that I learned his ways all those years ago.

3. What composers inspired you the most? Who is your favorite musician you have worked with?

These are two excellent questions. First, let's talk about the composers. When I was first learning about classical music, I listened to a lot of Brahms and Beethoven. These are two of the great romantic composers who share the sound of a full orchestra as well as a rhythmic drive that embraced me. Moving to the 20th century, I fell in love with Bartók and Stravinsky; talk about rhythm! These two were among the leaders to innovate rhythm, and as a percussionist, I was incredibly attracted and curious about their output.

That said, there were dozens of other composers who had significant influence on me for many different reasons. However, if I had to choose one composer who has had the most profound impact on me, I would have to say it is Gustav Mahler.

I could write a thesis on Mahler and how his music has impacted generations of musicians and non-musicians alike. Among his most significant works are his symphonies, and at the top of his symphonic offerings is *Symphony No. 2*, titled "The Resurrection Symphony." Here Mahler combines singers and instrumentalists to deepen his truly thoughtful writing. To help heighten the "Resurrection" experience, Mahler uses the first eight lines of text from the poem *Die Auferstehung* by Friedrich Gottlieb Klopstock in the finale of the symphony:

Rise again, yes, rise again,
Will you My dust,
After a brief rest!
Immortal life! Immortal life
Will He who called you, give you.
To bloom again were you sown!
The Lord of the harvest goes
And gathers in, like sheaves,
Us together, who died.

As you could imagine, the power of the words alone grabbed me with all the force a budding musician hungered for. Those words, coupled with the entrancing music, filled with thick scoring, rhythmic drive, and longing for all of eternity, punctuated by the lyrics, you too would be as enlightened as I was upon hearing this masterpiece.

As for my favorite musician I had ever worked with...Oh, my goodness, this is a complicated question for me to answer. Every soloist or act I have performed with has been a sincere blessing. All are worthy of the highest remarks, all made their impact on my life as an artist and my very soul as a human.

I have had the great pleasure to work with many sides of the musical spectrum, from classical music to pop and rock. It seems that the artists I love the most are often the ones I worked with most recently.

Roger Daltrey and Pete Townshend from the rock group The Who were among the nicest, most professional, relaxed, easy-going duo I could have ever hoped to work with.

The most self-confident appearing person I experienced was Hugh Jackman, another consummate professional. Hugh and I had many exchanges over the months where we worked. He always started our conversations by making a joke or sharing something of a light nature, always seemingly preparing me for some catastrophic news! Well, he never delivered such words, which made me quickly understand there was no hidden agenda, just a lovely man who cared about those with whom he was working.

The Game of Thrones tour placed me with my old friend and composer of the GoT experience, Ramin Djawadi. Ramin is another example of a kind, caring, non-aggressive musician in the midst of touring. I love working with him and his crew.

To answer your question, I need to say there is not one person or act I favor more than the other. I would like to reiterate it is an absolute blessing to work with the talent I have been afforded during my career. This may be my third book's topic, so keep your eye out for that sometime before 2022.

4. Where did you start to work with music? (Which employers hired you?)

My first "gig" as a musician was with the New York Youth symphony. Of course, there was no pay, but the reward for winning the principal timpani chair with three performances at Carnegie Hall was an unbelievable accomplishment. These performances took place when I was just 18 years old, and I will never forget each of them.

My first job for hire was with an organization called LOOM, or Light Opera of Manhattan.

LOOM performed a series of Gilbert and Sullivan operettas—it was great work! I got to perform on timpani as well as assorted percussion instruments. Nearly directly after being appointed to this position, the work doors opened up, and I found myself suddenly in high demand. My Mannes years were perhaps the most remarkable years of my younger life. Those years helped set the stage for what was about to happen. And what took place in my later college years propelled me into the workforce.

5. What would you tell college students like me who have some music background?

For anyone who listens to music, classical, rock, jazz, or other, I suggest listening with entirely open and innocent ears. I mean by innocent ears to listen with new, unfiltered ears, ears without prejudgment whatsoever. Allow the newness of music to flow over you—expose yourself to music you never heard before, try something new for a change!

Please remain open to not only music, but to everything that you know, but mostly for those things you have not yet experienced. I find those experiences to be the hidden charms in life.

Discovery is the joy of my life, and if I could have one wish, it would be for all to enjoy discovering newness together. I have had the happiness of finding relationships, relationships with friends, colleagues, wife, and children in my life. I have enjoyed the discovery of travel; the marvels of the world are at our disposal. The discovery of the arts, including dance, song, cinema, literature, and symphonic offerings, all left an impact. I have been blessed to discover the goodness of those with whom my path crossed: the multitudes of musicians, artists, managers, teachers, and all others who fill our world with wonder.

I strongly suggest to all: never give up on discovering all that has not yet been revealed. In those discoveries, you will find some of the greatest mysteries of life. Keep your mind open to everything and everyone; the truth is waiting to be discovered, and now it is time for your discovery!

A NEW BEGINNING

"Luck is where preparation meets opportunity."
–Roman philosopher Seneca

October turned into November, and Thanksgiving was quickly approaching. The symphony had extended my work through the end of November. By now, I had lived the past fifty or so days at the Omni Hotel and worked hard to get the personnel office train back on track. During this time, I began to build relationships with many: the music director, our CEO, the principal of each section, our concertmaster, but perhaps most importantly, the chairperson of the orchestra committee.

A large part of personnel management is based on relationship building. Building relationships isn't something that comes out of thin air; it is a real art to develop and own. The personnel manager is in a position to help both the orchestra members and their employer build a secure bridge of trust together. Sometimes, perhaps more often than not, there is a lack of trust between the two due to failed negotiations, misunderstandings, misguided feelings, and even desperation. I feel it is incumbent on the personnel manager to find a way to outwardly support both sides of the organization.

Moving toward a more harmonious relationship is like walking a constant and ever-evolving tightrope—one which we walk daily, carefully balancing out one's needs versus one's desires.

By mid-November, I knew for sure that once again, I loved being an orchestra personnel manager, and I adored my work at the Jacksonville Symphony. The members of the operations department are all extremely competent, as are the members of the orchestra. The Operations department members are those with whom I work most directly. The principal librarian, the Director of Artistic Administration, the Manager of Artistic Operations, the Stage Manager and his associates are strong forces, competent, and generous personalities. All those offices are managed or overseen by the General Manager, my friend and colleague who brought me to Jacksonville a few months earlier. These factors all seeped into my daily life, nightly dreams, and now, aspirations.

When I accepted the position as interim personnel manager, I told the general manager to post the opening on the appropriate websites as I was not interested in the full-time job. My family is up north in New Jersey, and I was not about to relocate us down south.

Before Thanksgiving, the general manager stopped by my office to say "good-bye" as he was heading home to New York for the holidays. His announcement made me feel unsettled, in fact, uncomfortable with the thought of leaving to go back home permanently in a few days myself.

Truly conflicted and feeling torn between going back home to my family and wanting to continue my current position, I asked the general manager if he would like to discuss the position more. His response was, "you have not applied, so there isn't much to discuss." At that moment, just as he was exiting the building, I jotted him an email:

"Dear General Manager, I would like to apply for the Orchestra Personnel Managers position with the Jacksonville Symphony Association. Attached is my resume for your consideration."

Until I officially applied for the position, there was nothing to discuss, and rightfully so. I began to think, what happens if they offer me the job? What then? Because I felt the success of my first two months and renewed hope in my life, I knew it was time to start thinking about the terms of a possible agreement.

The job was the topic of conversation between my wife and me over the next week. The burning focus remained about me feeling complete, working again in a classical orchestra setting, and the need for steady work. The wonderful possibility of working in Florida was only deflated by the thought of being away from my home in New Jersey, my wife, our sons, and my life as I have known it for fifty-three years.

I felt rejuvenated and selfish in each conversation, but because of my partner's laser focus and understanding, we made it through each call. I had no idea what was waiting for me but knew the answer was just over the horizon. I asked my wife, "what are we going to do if they accept my terms?" Her reply was short but powerful, "you will accept it, and we will figure out the rest together."

After negotiating my employment terms, and a series of interviews during the week of Thanksgiving, on 1 December 2018, we reached an agreement. Although this was a bittersweet moment in our lives, we were most grateful for the opportunity to be reemployed in the industry. Additionally, I was reunited with an old colleague and accepted by the Jacksonville family's various factions. The membership seemed to embrace me, and I desired to remain part of this caring organization.

Shortly after accepting the position, I moved to solidify my relationship in a few critical, but welcome, meetings with the orchestra committee chair. My deal was simple; let's trust each other until either of us shows we can no longer maintain that trust. Our relationship and goodwill work both ways, and without hesitation, we both agreed to the proposition. To this day, we have not looked back. Our current committee chair is a stand-up guy, with a strong personality. Yet, I do not find him to be a strongly opinionated person as he is open to all discussions, and possibilities. Those qualities only benefit a true leader, and for me, it is a true blessing to be working with him.

The downside of accepting the job has to do with my internal struggle. That struggle became apparent shortly after digesting my new position and location. I felt I was living the supreme juxtaposition: happiness in my new job and loneliness away from my family. I shared the news with my oldest brother, Joe, who I look to for counsel and sound advice. Drawing on his past experiences, he demonstrated complete understanding as he shared his views on the difficulties of living apart from my family. He understood the desire and the need to reconnect, to feel relevant in my work. He was careful to advise but also offered a window into some waiting struggles.

I can't help but think how my life parallels that of Francesco. We share a devotion to music, along with the internal struggles over our personal needs versus those of our family. In both instances, our strong connection to our art has pushed us to move where we found work and where we were accepted. Additionally, both of us had the support of our spouses, who have stood by our side.

AND THEN, COVID-19 HIT

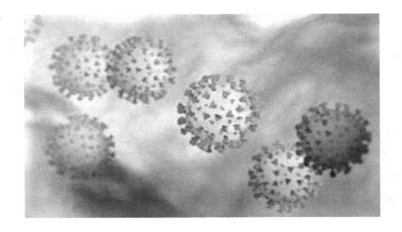

"If I cease searching, then, woe is me, I am lost. That is how
I look at it—keep going, keep going, come what may."
–Vincent van Gogh

On 14 March 2020, at 8:01 p.m., the General Manager of the
Jacksonville Symphony walked into my office. The orchestra had just
finished tuning, and we were about to perform a virtual concert. Only
one day prior, the Mayor of Jacksonville, Lenny Curry, confirmed the
closing of the Times-Union Center for the Performing Arts building.
Since its conception in mid-1995, the Times-Union Center for the
Performing Arts has been owned and run by the City of Jacksonville.

He looked me in the eyes and said, "I want you to pack up your
office and go home." I replied, "home, to Riverside?" He told me, "no,
to your home in New Jersey." COVID-19 was all of a sudden real, and
it hit us hard.

Our Florida condo is located in the charming town of Riverside, just three miles from the Times-Union Center for the Performing Arts building. Riverside and Avondale are adjacent neighborhoods in central Jacksonville. Although residential, the two towns are considered one; the area boasts a gorgeous commercial district that includes Five Points, the King Street District, and Avondale's unique shops. Riverside, first mapped out in 1868, was annexed by Jacksonville in 1887. Today, the area is known for its diverse architecture and historic preservation.

I powered down my laptop and packed my satchel with about three inches of "active" files sitting on my desk. As I reached my office door, before turning off the light, I gave the room the once over to see if there was anything else I should consider taking with me. I thought it might be a few weeks before I would return, so I grabbed all the payroll files that sit to the immediate right of my desk, on the middle shelf of a six-shelf bookcase. I pushed the weighted block that keeps the door propped open with my right foot, and in one movement, the door closed as I shut off the lights.

Before leaving the building, I walked to the stage, watched, and listened. It was a surreal moment. I never thought, in my lifetime, I would witness such a thing. The orchestra performed in front of live cameras that sent our music out over the internet. The house, however, was empty. That vision would remain emblazoned in my mind for what turned out to be many months.

As I crossed back to the exit door, I could hear the clicking of my shoes on the corridor floor. Click-clop, click-clop—the sound resonated in my ears as I reached the front door. The sound continued on the outside pavement all the way to my car, which was parked in the lot across the street. As I stepped outside, I felt the chilly, 63° air shower over me. I remember thinking how much I love winters in Florida, protected from the snow and cold weather up north. Everything seemed to be magnified, my steps, the air, and my emotions.

As I got into my car, I placed my iPhone on the magnetic holder and started the engine. Once the power was on, Bluetooth˚ kicked in, and my phone began to play music. Music filled the car and my ears as I prepared for my short, three-mile journey home.

I parked my car in my designated spot, A13. I had made the same travel plans dozens of times over the past 18 months. Park, pack, prepare, fly, and return. Just as there was a rhythm with my work, there was also a rhythm to my routine. But this time, it felt different because this trip to New Jersey was open-ended. I needed to consider purchasing a one-way ticket and then wait to see when things would ease up before returning.

Upon entering our condo, I placed my work ID badge, which had been dangling around my neck, in the glass bowl that sits on our mid-eastern table in the foyer. I kicked my shoes off and attached my New Jersey keys to my travel bag with the waiting carabiner key ring. One significant advantage of owning two homes is I don't need to pack much when traveling. There was no need for toiletries, clothes, or nearly anything else. I had the art of traveling down to a science.

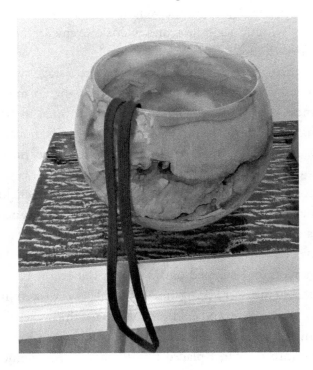

Glass bowl in the foyer of our Florida condo

I sat down in my home office, booted up the laptop, and went to the familiar website, Google Travel. I entered all the possible criteria for the first flight out in the morning and found a 9:15 a.m. flight with open seats. I purchased a one-way ticket, and after doing so, I called my wife to share the events of the evening. She was relieved to hear I was coming home, especially under the generally unknown circumstances at that time.

I went into my closet and grabbed my travel bag. Along with my work laptop and files, I placed my earbuds, passport, battery for recharging my phone, USB cable, and adaptor. I then called my colleague from the symphony, who lives just a few blocks from me, and shared my open-ended plan with him. My colleague, one of the kindest people I have ever known, assured me not to worry and that in my absence, he would look after the condo and my car.

When traveling back and forth to New Jersey, I consider taking an Uber to the airport, just 15 miles away. Parking is an unbelievably low cost of $6 per day in the "long term" parking lot. This parking lot is within walking distance to the airport but provides a shuttle service every 8-10 minutes, so there was no need to hike over.

On all trips of eight days or less, I would park my car at the airport, but for longer trips, around Christmas and Easter, I would take an Uber. The cost is around $25 one way. I did the math, and $50 was the magic equation that worked for me. The only other variable is my ability to drive on my schedule if I drove myself or being at the mercy of when an Uber would arrive to pick me up. Uber is generally available any time of the day or night, though.

Most of my direct flights to Newark International Airport depart at 6 a.m., which would require me to leave no later than 4:45 a.m. If I needed an Uber, I would set my request for 4:30 a.m. I never had issues with Uber or Lyft; both are consistently smooth and reliable.

The one enormous advantage to waking up so early is that I would be in New Jersey with my wife and son in time for their morning coffee. The total round-trip time, Florida condo door to New Jersey condo door would never exceed four hours and fifteen minutes; not so bad!

By now, it was close to 11 p.m., and I had just a few hours to grab some shut-eye. After double-checking the contents of my travel bag, I poured a nightcap then hit the bed.

Alexa announced it was time to get up; I did, but unlike most other early morning alarms, I sprung out of bed without effort, as getting home was my paramount concern. After a brief shower, I asked Alexa, "play the news." This was part of my daily routine and rhythm. The news reported on just one topic for the few minutes I was listening: COVID-19.

The Uber arrived, and off we went. I felt I was traveling into uncertainty, as COVID-19 was the talk of the nation. Those who were flying that morning were more apprehensive than usual. I completely understood as I felt the same trepidation as the rest of the passengers on flight UA 3418. When booking airline tickets, I always do my best to be in the front of the aircraft. 3A is my usual seat assignment, which is the first row in coach and comes at a lower cost than a first-class ticket price for the one hour and forty-two minute flight.

On the flight, there were many travelers clutching bottles of sanitizer, and most were wearing facemasks. Sanitizer, facemasks, and social distancing were all later discussed as scientific preventers of the spread of COVID-19. Although we were just at the beginning of the pandemic, there was fear in the air. It was unmistakable, palpable, and frightening. The fear of the unknown to me is the worst fear I could suffer. We could not see the looming enemy but felt like it was hovering over us all the time.

As the aircraft began to taxi for take-off, my mind began to wander. Usually, I would be overly concerned about the actual flight itself; I suffer from post-traumatic stress over flying since the terrorist attack back on 9/11. On this flight, my attention was focused on what was to come next. What is next? I asked myself over and over. How do we, as musicians, enter the stage again and perform for hundreds, if not thousands, of patrons?

Over the past decades, I have lived a life where there was no I, me, or mine, but for the first time in my memory, I could not erase the possibility that "I" might be one who suffers from the virus. My work at the large concert hall events, arena productions, and my work in Jacksonville would suffer; all these contribute to our comfortable lifestyle. As the plane picked up speed and left the ground, my eyes began to well up. I was deeply in pain, pain from my very selfish concern for me, not the world at large. I was concerned about my livelihood, comfort, needs, desire, and work. I was a mess.

In the months that followed, all of my fears became realities. I, along with millions of others, was subject to the plague which surrounded our daily lives. The difference between now, and that horrible flight home from Jacksonville, is that I have a deeper understanding of what we are up against. There is still little I can do, but I was able to place myself back to where I am more considerate of others than myself.

LIFE IN LEGNANO

"Vision is the art of seeing what is invisible to others."
–Jonathan Swift

During his failed attempt to jumpstart his career in Vanzago, Francesco met Giovanni Borioli, by chance. Borioli, who lived in Legnano, was a municipal councilor. Borioli offered him the position as director of the Amici dell'Arte Society of Legnano, a fabulous choir. Francesco accepted his generous offer and, in September 1921, moved himself and his family for the last time to the beautiful northern Italian city of Legnano.

He was readmitted as an honorary member to the German Society of Authors, which was suspended since the outbreak of the First World War. Just one month after relocating to Legnano, with the support of Borioli, he obtained the post of German Language teacher at the Municipal Technical Institute. The institute was government-run and committed to bringing the Society of the Friends of Art of Legnano to a high artistic level.

As Francesco solidified his position, he formed an orchestra and gave numerous concerts. He and the orchestra performed most of the Beethoven Symphonies. He also organized opera performances of Bellini's *Norma*, Verdi's *Ernani*, and Donizetti's *Lucia di Lammermoor*, which were also given in the neighboring municipalities of Saronno, Magenta, Castellanza, and Busto Arsizio.

Francesco's accomplishments and success were well recognized, and he quickly established himself as a musical force.

During this time, his first review in this new position helped bring his name to the forefront.

On 6 November 1922, *La Nonna in Busto Arsizio, in "Il Seco lo XIX di Milano" wrote:*

"From the beginning, the conductor of the orchestra has been deserving of praise and commendation. He has succeeded in using the elements he had at his disposal (the orchestra of Legnano and the choir of Busto Arsizio) to obtain a harmonic fusion and perfection. And to overcome the many technical difficulties that the score presents. In a word, Bravo, Maestro Neglia."

On 3 December 1921, the first vocal-instrumental competition of the Society took place, and a week later, Francesco was appointed choir director of the Rossini Choral Society of Busto Arsizio.

After only six months of living in Legnano, he obtained two fellowships. The first of these fellowships was in Rescaldina (1922/23), and the second was about twenty kilometers outside of Milan, in Cerro Maggiore (October 1924 to March 1926). At the Popular University of Legnano, Busto Arsizio, and Monza, Francesco also held several cultural conferences and showcased chamber music performances. At these conferences, Francesco would often perform as a violin soloist.

While his artistic life took hold, a black cloud darkened over the Neglia household. His wife became stricken with an incurable disease. When Maria's sickness first set in, she refrained from complaining, as she did not wish to distract her husband from his life mission. But soon, she became immobile and remained in that condition for just over a year. She followed her husband's activities with great interest and even kept in touch via letter correspondences with relatives, friends, and admirers in Hamburg.

Sadly, on 29 January 1923, Maria died in Legnano. The Marquis Pappalepore, Consul of Hamburg, and later Minister Plenipotentiary wrote a letter on this sad occasion, which gives us an idea of the moral character of Francesco's dear wife, Maria.

Rome, 2 February 1923

"Dear friend,

The bad news that your correspondence brings has deeply dismayed all of us, and we join our tears to reflect your most bitter loss.

Poor Signora Neglia was an angel of goodness and an exemplary wife and mother. We still have emblazoned in our minds all the happiness she had when her devoted husband presented himself to the applause of the audience.

When the time has eased your great pain, I hope you will write to me, making me aware of the successes that undoubtedly await you in the course of your life.

In the meantime, dear Professor, always have me in your heart together with my wife. She has always remained your admirer and sends you all the condolences that pervade our souls for their irreparable misfortune.

Always affectionate about you, Pappalepore."

After two years of solitude, Francesco married Teresa Rotharmel, also of German descent, and had a son, Francesco Jr., nicknamed Franco.

Francesco with second wife, Teresa Rotharmel and son, Franco.
photo credits Laura Fusaro, *Maestro sul podio e nella vita*

Ten months later, on 31 October 1923, Francesco presented his symphonic suite *Three Paintings of Venetian Life* in the competition organized by "Musica d'oggi" of the Casa Ricordi for symphonic works. The commission was formed by Franco Alfano, Ildebrando Pizzetti, and Arturo Toscanini, who expressed themselves in the following way:

The Commission has diligently examined the works submitted. Nine pieces of which we report the title and motive according to the order of presentation seemed worthy of a second examination, namely the following: Overture for Cyrano; Epic Vision; Dream of Promised Land; Landscape Impressions; **Three Venetian Paintings***: Spring of Dreams; Don Quixote; Suite in Four Times, and Bachiana Orgy.*

On 10 February 1924, Francesco obtained a transfer to Cerro Maggiore and began teaching music in a class of sixty students. In his year-end report, he wrote: "I was able to teach easy 2-part songs to my pupils. A 'Hymn to the Flag' composed by me to the words of Caval Lotti." His pupils learned and soon loved the hymn. The hymn was heard being sung on the streets of Cerro Maggiore by all who lived in the village.

FRANCESCO PAOLO NEGLIA

" THREE PICTURES OF VENETIAN LIFE ,,

SYMPHONICAL SUITE - OP. 32

CONDUCTED BY
HERBERT ALBERT
with the
Great Symphonical Orchestra of R. A. I. of Turin

Francesco's *Three Venetian Paintings* ultimately
claimed first prize in the Ricordi competition

While in Cerro Maggiore, Francesco organized a large celebration
concert for the Italian flag and heritage. The celebration was such a
success that on 4 March 1926, he was in high demand from the city of
Legnano and once again moved back. He was entrusted to teach the

highest level of music classes, which included vocal direction to the upper levels in all Legnano schools, an enormous accomplishment.

Francesco's good fortune turned from the difficult years before Maria's death to current times where he was gaining success. Although the success he was living did not entirely live up to his Hamburg days, his success was noteworthy, and respectable to say the very least.

BATTLING THE PANDEMIC

"Victory awaits him who has everything in order—luck we call it. Defeat is definitely due for him who has neglected to take the necessary precautions—bad luck we call it" –Roald Amundsen

When I agreed to the position in Jacksonville, part of that agreement was that I would have the flexibility to work from my New Jersey home whenever the orchestra was not on stage. The freedom to travel would allow me to spend time with my wife and sons during the year. If we were off for even two days, I would fly home. Although the symphony was working 38 contiguous weeks, there was still plenty of time to make travel plans. Examining the orchestra's work schedule, I began to make travel arrangements.

In my first year with the orchestra, Sasha and I took about four months to get into our travel rhythm. The one thing we discovered was that we had about an 18-day threshold for being apart. After 18 days, we became less tolerant of our current situation and forced a brief, but meaningful, rendezvous.

Having summers up north with my family was a blessing, yet it made it more challenging to return to Florida in September. After 12 glorious weeks home, settling into my old rhythm with our sons and home life, in general, was a true blessing. I began to think of it as something to look forward to, as opposed to something I would have to do without for the long fall and winter months.

Our first 15-16 months worked as planned, and we were content with our newly found visit timeline. Then the pandemic hit, and I was sent home unexpectedly. Although I was beyond happy to be reunited with my family much earlier than expected, there was a dark cloud looming over us, all of us.

The pandemic was spiraling out of control, and there was no leadership coming from the government to speak of. As a result, it was up to each state to make decisions regarding opening. We learned later that these decisions appeared to have been solely based on what is now understood to be highly politicized reasons.

As the pandemic ravaged the country, and the world, by the summer of 2020, just a few months after learning about COVID-19, the governor of the state of Florida announced that they would be open for business come the summer.

I was in disbelief; how could it be? What was the rationale of the governor? It certainly wasn't based on any of the scientific reports flooding the media for months. All I can think is that he would be playing a game of political suicide to remain closed, so conversely, he played life and death with the inhabitants of the Sunshine State. This was a deplorable, selfish act in my eyes.

Now it was up to me to decide if I would be returning to work in the fall.

We, as an organization, had to figure out not only if we should open in September, but if we do, how do we do so safely?

An October 2020 journal entry of mine shares what took place before returning, and then upon returning, to work:

Journal Entry: 13 October 2020 11:52 p.m.
Eight months into the pandemic:

> *I am reliving an earlier conversation with a colleague who works in one of the major orchestras; we spoke of our current situation, both vastly different. We had just learned that a New York orchestra had canceled the entire 20-21 season, and both felt that decision could set a ripple effect throughout Lincoln Center, as well as the New York metropolitan area. However, although we are reduced to one-third of the seating in Jacksonville, we are open for business.*

The conversation danced from disbelief to actuality. Many organizations were canceling all live performances; both large and small orchestras felt the unthinkable impact of the pandemic. Meanwhile, the Jacksonville Symphony moved forward with a live audience and up to 53 members on the stage sharing music with all those who wish to listen.

During our discussion, we agreed that we were both placed in a difficult situation. Unemployment is the worst possible outcome. Not having money to pay rent, mortgage, taxes, power, cable, cell phone, toilet paper, and more, were all extremely painful, and stressful, but seemingly unavoidable.

I don't want this to sound arrogant, as I feel blessed to be working, but conversely, going to work every day had also proved extremely challenging. I felt responsible for keeping the musicians who were performing on stage safe. Along with them, we needed to consider the staff and patrons as well.

The lack of national leadership regarding COVID was astounding. Although scientists and professionals were united to find ways to mitigate COVID, we had zero information about safety and how we could proceed as a nation to finally get a grip on this dreadful virus. That highly politicized topping alone was what I believe led to the turning point, the changing of the guard. Ultimately, the people spoke, and the change was made.

We needed to act long before the government could, so we went to work. During the summer of 2020, when we were trying to figure out how to return to work safely, I, along with the orchestra committee and senior staff at the symphony, spent countless hours learning about aerosol emissions. We would join the endless number of web seminars offered to understand better the safety issues surrounding us.

Armed with a great deal of positive knowledge, we presented our findings to the membership, staff, and symphony board. When I refer to "we," I am referring to those of us who are in a position to discuss a path forward and make binding decisions to proceed safely. That group consists of the Orchestra Committee, who are a group of elected musicians to represent the entirety of the orchestra; the

American Federation of Musicians, Local 444; the governing body of the membership of the symphony; The International Alliance of Theatrical Stage Employees, IATSE Local 115; and, of course, the management of the symphony itself. Each of these groups added to a working document on safety at the symphony.

We zoomed, used Google documents, and chatted on the phone to drill down on each detail of concern. Once we were all in agreement with the document's wording, we were able to move forward. Creating the document was a crucially important task that fell in our laps, and we needed to make sure every detail was discussed, tweaked as needed, and finally agreed upon.

The final document which was agreed upon by various factions of the organization included our complete and thorough safety protocol procedures. It discussed everything, including having symptoms, testing, rehearsal and performance protocols, distribution of music scores to the musicians of the orchestra, entering the building, social distancing, and more.

If you would like to see the entire, unabridged document, please see Appendix II.

Regardless of all the safety concerns and agreements, I was not able to get beyond my issues. Every day that I showed up to work, I was frightened. I was concerned about the safety of all the musicians, staff, and patrons constantly. I couldn't concentrate on nearly anything, as I was consumed with thoughts of safety. I didn't know if I was nuts or on the mark; I had no barometer by which to gauge myself. Insanity prevailed, with no clear direction out. I hoped that when there was a vaccine, I would begin to feel differently, but that seemed to be a long way away.

Journal Entry: 14 December 2020, 1:59 p.m.

We have come a long way since my entry on 13 October 2020. I am happy to share that we have not had one case of COVID in our orchestra or staff. There also seems to be a light at the end of this very dark tunnel. The vaccine was rolled out today in the United States. Although we have a long way to go, I am starting to feel encouraged by the possibility of a more normal life in the months to come.

On 31 January 2021, one of my colleagues from another orchestra contacted me with a question. It read in part:

"I was asked to see if I could drum up any existing language which was used if a concert/week/or partial week was canceled due to a COVID positive test result by a musician or guest artist who has already started services that week. We are trying to get ahead of the game when we need to cancel anything under those circumstances. Is there any language you used to send to the orchestra you would be willing to share with us?"

A few minutes later I replied:

Unfortunately, we needed to cancel a performance a few weeks ago. I, like you, wanted to stay ahead of this possibility as I felt, at some point, we were going to need it.

Once I learned who tested positive for COVID, I called that person and began my contact tracing duties. It turns out that he, the soloist, never had anyone visit him in his dressing room (which would be against our COVID safety plan in place). However, one of our staff members had dinner with him the night before, and that staff person was in my office for over an hour on the day of the canceled concert. The staff person and I quarantined for the recommended period. Before returning to work, we both had two negative COVID tests over five days.

Before sending out the email below, I called my concertmaster, principal 2ⁿᵈ, and music director and had them quarantined as well. All were close enough to the soloist that we chose to take extreme caution. Although all were wearing masks and seated six feet apart, we still had them quarantined.

We felt it was imperative to call any musicians before sending the email out for obvious reasons. Once I sent the email out, my phone began ringing off the hook. Because I did the contact tracing and had already informed those who might have been exposed, I shared with each musician who called that they were not in any danger whatsoever.

Most, if not all, were comforted by our process and how well we were prepared for this possibility. I felt it was my duty to keep everyone calm and reassure them there was nothing to fear.

I sent this email to the membership:

Dear Orchestra Members,

We have learned that a person who was present in Jacoby Hall during Friday evening's performance has since tested positive for COVID. Out of an abundance of caution, we have decided to cancel tonight's concert.

If the Personnel Manager has not contacted you, you were not considered to have been in close proximity to the affected person.

Thank you for the hard work and dedication you've shown in following our safety protocols. We should all be proud of that accomplishment.

We will stay closely in touch and let you know of any developments.

The email proved to be helpful, and I was glad to have done my homework in advance. We take COVID very seriously and need to ensure as full protection as possible for all who enter our hall.

Journal entry: 6 June 2021, 4:54 p.m.

We have completed 37 contiguous weeks of performing and have one more to go before the 2020-2021 season has officially ended. I am happy to share that the symphony has performed for more than 42,000 patrons, and during the season, we have not had one reported case of COVID-19 from our patrons. In addition, not one of our staff or musicians has been infected by COVID, a truly remarkable bit of news.

I have felt for many months that the law of averages was against us, and sooner or later, we would need to close our doors. Although there were weeks, if not months, of nervousness, concern, and even fear, we, as an organization, embraced our safety protocols and showed the entire music community how to get on stage and perform safely.

I am immensely proud of the superb leadership of the Jacksonville Symphony administration, as much as I am of the musicians who believe in working together to share our number one gift, the gift of live music! Tutti Bravi!

ROYAL CARIBBEAN

"The greatest wealth is to live content with little, for there
is never want where the mind is satisfied." –Lucretius

When the casinos were opening in Atlantic City during the 1970s,
they took a page from Las Vegas's casino trade's book. The hotel and
casino business had concentrated their efforts on attracting gamblers to
their establishments. Before long, all establishments were in harmony
in their approach; each would focus on bringing the best entertainment
into the casino, attracting potential gamblers to come and hear a
performance from well-known personalities.

In turn, the cruise industry operated as the casinos did. The cruise
company would send recruiters to sign onto their performance roster
the most talented and gifted musicians they could find. Once Royal
Caribbean Group heard of Maria, she quickly became one of those they
considered a must-have, as she was considered the best of the best. The
top recruiters fell in love with Maria, her act, and her exuberant attitude.

Around 1975, Maria started her transition from the television,
nightclub, and even presidential appearances she had enjoyed for decades
to a more focused platform aboard the Royal Caribbean, Norwegian,
and Alaskan Cruises lines, among others. She worked as an entertainer
in the cruise industry for the next 30-plus years, until her retirement in
2012, at the age of 83. During that time, Maria was the headliner, the
talent that all had come to see.

Maria Neglia at 80 years young.

Draped in glittering sequined gowns, she would take the stage twice a day to entertain the eager audiences. She performed her musical arrangements of the *Root Beer Rag, A Fifth of Beethoven, Hot Canary, You Light Up My Life, All I Ask/Memory Medley, Orange Blossom Special,* and an amazingly entertaining medley from *Fiddler on the Roof* she used as her encore. Her performances were loved and talked about from the moment the last note was played. An infectious buzz would run through the ship, alerting those who missed her performance to get in line for the next one.

Maria also possessed an extremely witty sense of humor, never missing the opportunity to crack a joke. An audience member noted that during one of her performances Maria had a slight mishap, resulting in an impromptu comment. Just after playing the opening cadenza of *Fiddler on the Roof,* one of the strings on her violin snapped. It happened to be her "G" string. She quickly reacted to the situation by stating to the audience, "Well, ladies and gentlemen, my G-string has snapped, so I must go!" It was reported that the audience broke into laughter because they thought she meant she wore a G-string!

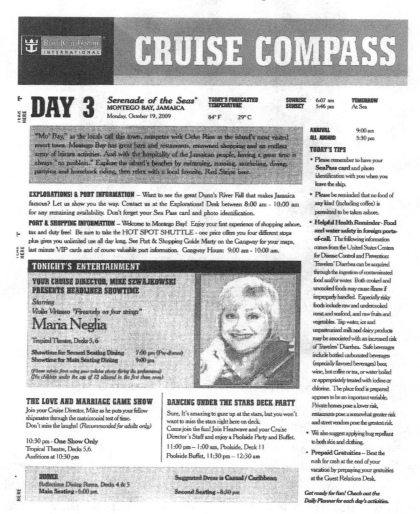

Maria as Top Talent on Royal Caribbean

Maria loved to socialize with the passengers and with the other acts that were performing on the cruise with her. She loved the mystery of travel and always disembarked the ship when entering a new city. She loved exploring her new surroundings, culture, people, and cuisine.

Marty Allen, American comedian and actor,
along with his wife, Karon Blackwell

Royal Caribbean offered her the headliner spot and a large, comfortable suite that befitted her extraordinary talents. A normal workweek for my aunt would include practicing in her cabin suite. She would rehearse with the accompanying ensemble, generally a 12-piece band, the day before her performances. She was a perfectionist and wanted to share only the best she and her band could offer her public. She was very direct and demanding of her musicians in rehearsals and performances. Her product had to rise to an extremely high level, or she would share her dissatisfaction with her bandmates and scrap a tune that might not be working up to her expected level.

Maria with comedian Ronnie Martin

Maria was treated like absolute gold on the ship. Every crew member, staff, and traveler knew her and loved her, and Maria loved being loved.

During one of her performances, the lighting and smoke designs were not functioning to her expectations. At one point, she shouted from the stage to the technician, "You're choking me, darling! Jesus! Enough smoke!" The audience ate it up, and ultimately, Maria got what she needed, less smoke.

One of her favorite outfits was a blue sequined dress. At times during her performances when wearing that dress, she would joke with the audience about wearing her "Blue-light, K-Mart special." She knew how to wow the audience, not only with her impeccable performances but also with her clever banter on stage. She was often referred to as the "Female Victor Borge."

Maria with singer, songwriter, and pianist Bobby Arvon

Reviews and comments left on the various cruise line comments pages included many complimentary messages for Maria.

On 5 March 2006, one passenger commented on the ship's online blog: "Has anyone else seen the violinist Maria Neglia? If so, what did you think?" The responses came pouring in; all had the same sentiments, which I will consolidate and paraphrase:

> I absolutely fell in love with her and her talent. And she is *such* a character. We saw her on Jewel of the Seas in September on a ten-night cruise. She was the featured entertainment on the second night of entertainment. I know she stayed on board the rest of the cruise because we kept running into her. I can only guess she is in her 70s and about three and a half feet tall. She is extremely funny, but moreover, MAN CAN SHE PLAY! I ended up buying her CD, and I still listen to it in my car regularly. I would almost book another cruise because I knew she would be on, but I don't think there is any way to find out ahead of time which entertainers will

be featured on board? I am sure she cruises other lines, but I hope and hope I come across her again someday!

Fred Travalena, an American entertainer specializing in comedy and impressions

Another passenger commented:

We have seen her on a couple of cruises. She certainly is one of a kind. We enjoyed her act, and she is definitely a very talented violinist.

On 24 April 2010, when Maria was 82, other passengers shared their thoughts which read in part:

We just saw Maria Neglia on the Radiance, and she was fantastic. I, too, wish there was a way to find out what the entertainment will be on the ships in advance, but half the fun is the surprise element. I guess you could find some of her schedule by going to her fansite. I've read that she's in

her 80's. If so, I wish I had half her energy. If you get a chance to see her perform, don't miss her show.

I saw Maria Neglia on the Enchantment in March 2011 on a nine-night cruise from Baltimore. She brought down the house. My companion remembers seeing her on the Ed Sullivan show.

Yes, we saw her a couple of years ago. We thought she was fantastic. Many fellow cruisers decided not to attend because they didn't like the violin. After the show, they were sorry when they heard how entertaining she was.

We saw her later at the Vancouver Airport with her sixteenth-century Amati violin strapped to her back. She was a pleasure to hear, and absolutely, an unforgettable performance.

June Valli (center), American singer and television personality, with husband Jimmy Merchant

Royal Caribbean International boasted that the hit of the week was the virtuoso violinist Maria Neglia, billed as "Fireworks on Four Strings;" she typically received three standing ovations. Accompanied by the Vision of the Seas Orchestra, she mesmerized the audience. People were talking about her for the rest of the cruise. She comes from a long line of musicians, and it shows!

Maria, with President Jimmy Carter

In 2015, I learned my aunt's health was declining. Although I had not seen her in a long time, I purchased an airline ticket to travel from Newark International Airport in New Jersey to Waco Regional Airport in Texas via Dallas.

Although we hadn't set eyes on each other in nearly forty years, she recognized me immediately. We began to catch up on her deteriorating health and condition. We ultimately decided it was time to place all of her worldly possessions into my care. That meant taking her to a lawyer to sign a power of attorney, placing all she owned into my name. Once that was completed, I transferred everything she had just signed over to me to my half-sister, Dina. Though she now was living in Minnesota, Dina had lived across the street from Maria for most of her life and knew her much better than I.

Dina and I made all permanent arrangements for the remainder of our aunt's life. Dina was now in charge of paying all Maria's bills and living obligations.

I was able to arrange all of this in the 36 hours I had in Waco. Once I felt everything was in place, and before I left Waco, I called Dina. During our short but meaningful conversation, I shared that I didn't think Maria would survive another year. I struggled with my departure, as I knew in my heart this would be the last time I would set eyes on my aunt again.

Ten months later, I received the phone call. She was gone.

Thinking about the best resting place for her, a person who rarely called the house she lived in a home, it was decided the sea should be the final resting place of our nomadic aunt. The sea that she grew to love during the second part of her life is the same sea that now claimed her body, soul, and memories.

A week after her passing, Maria's ashes were spread over the scenic Red River in Fargo, North Dakota, a beautiful river that stretches to Canada. The Red River is a river in North America which flows primarily northward instead of southward.

Like Francesco, Maria endured many struggles. Although she enjoyed a busy and lucrative life, she was also conflicted with some life decisions. Maria desired a better balance between living on the road and the countless sacrifices while living on the great sea. Maria never married or raised a family and, like most successful traveling musicians, missed many family events. Birthdays, graduations, extended relationships with her nieces and nephews, and the comforts of home were mostly lost in her life as she sacrificed it all for the love of music.

Maria Neglia

AND IN THE END

"An Ego Mind is a destructive mind, and a rational mind is a peaceful mind" –Charleston Parker

On 10 December 1927, Francesco presented the first musical concert of the Musical Institute to the municipality of Legnano. Ten months later, on 2 October 1928, the mayor of Legnano, Commendatore Fabio Vignati, gathered the town council. The Commendatore and council unanimously agreed to open a musical high school for Francesco to run.

Just one month later, on 9 November 1929, the Giuseppe Verdi Civic Musical Liceo [High School] was inaugurated in Legnano. Classes began on 2 December with sixteen pupils, most of whom were Francesco's private pupils.

After word spread that the school was successful, the enrollment increased from sixteen to forty-nine students. The Liceo secured musicians such as Guglielmo Zuelli, the honorary inspector; Renzo Bossi, ministerial commissioner; Antonio Russolo; and Riccardo Malipiero, brother of the famous Gianfrancesco; to teach the newly expanded student body.

Liceo Concert –November 1929
photo credit *Maurizio* Agrò *Nella vita e nell'arte*

On 10 April 1930, Francesco organized a concert for the students of the Liceo. Among them was his daughter Emma, and his niece Maria Evelina, the daughter of his brother Liborio. Another daughter of Liborio who joined was Elena, who had been admitted to the honors class with the master, Russolo.

Liborio Neglia
photo credit: Laura Fusaro, *Maestro sul podio e nella vita*

Emma Neglia
photo credit: Laura Fusaro, *Maestro sul podio e nella vita*

Maria Evelina Neglia
photo credit: Laura Fusaro, *Maestro sul podio e nella vita*

By 1931 the musical high school had seventy students, and with the backing of the banks and industrialists of Legnano, scholarships were established to reward the best students. In the first year, the scholarships totaled £3,500. As director of the musical institute, Francesco not only took care of the artistic and teaching activities but also oversaw and implemented all financial decisions. He had already had experience running the Neglia Conservatorium in Hamburg.

His musical school had regular activities, and final exams were held for all courses. Musical preparations were based on the same level as the conservatories. In 1931, Eugenio Bonacina, a graduate of Music History under Francesco, was the first to be accepted into The Royal Conservatory of Milan.

Because the music high school was a private school, it became difficult for the children of poor families to attend. Francesco wrote a letter to the mayor asking for the recognition of the school. The management system of the Liceo was still based on the method of private lessons: more students meant more taxes and, therefore, more income for teachers; fewer students meant fewer taxes and consequently a smaller income.

On 12 December 1931, Neglia wrote to the podestà:

> *By giving the Liceo the guise of a Civic institution, it would have very little to spend. This would also serve to normalize its position vis-à-vis mobile wealth and citizenship....A municipal employee, perhaps ragioniere [accountant] Campanini, could examine everything related to the application of the proposed idea and establish the overall annual expenses of the school. I am sure that it will not inflate the municipal budget.*

Meanwhile, the artistic activity of the Liceo was becoming busier as Francesco organized a cycle of ten themed concerts. These concerts ranged from instrumental music of the 1600s to the music of living composers, a clear sign of the Maestro's constant musical evolution. Music by Zuelli, Malipiero, Russolo, Pizzetti, Brogi, and, of course, his own music was performed.

The necessary money was raised to allow the enrollment of the less fortunate to attend the school. Soon performances throughout the municipality were performed. Everything in Francesco's life was progressing favorably, and he was on the cusp of gaining the same success and notoriety he had enjoyed in Hamburg.

The pupils of the school pose in front of the Teatro
Legnano after a performance –1930
Photo credit Laura Fusaro, *Maestro sul podio e nella vita*

On the heels of this unimaginable, yet determined, comeback, his health began to deteriorate.

In 1931, Francesco began to experience the onset of nephritis, which is inflammation of the kidneys. He was advised to rest for at least a month to help cure his ailment.

He wrote to his children from his home in Legnano on 14 December 1931. These letters were preserved and later shared by his son, Peppino, before his death in 1974.

> *Beloved children,*
> *The days go by; indeed, they fly, and fortunately, in the heat of my work, I can hardly notice my pain. I don't have time to get sick, but I complain of fatigue and heaviness in my head. Patience, I must be patient! I feel a bit of guilt as I always take things too zealously. I went to teach at school and intended to share a lesson, but I forgot what I intended to teach when I stood in front of the students. While I speak, I cry inside as I feel threatened by my sickness.*

Francesco always kept himself calm, serene, and without allowing his good-natured and habitual humor to abandon him. Unfortunately, the symptoms took hold. Francesco wrote to Peppino to share the inevitable.

Legnano, 2 January 1932

> *They say that I am sick and have to stay at home, limit myself to milk, and eat potatoes, pasta with milk, and cooked fruit and vegetables in oil. We will see, after ten days, if the treatment and the punishment of confinement will help my recovery.*

A few weeks later, on 15 January 1932, he wrote:

Peppino,
Unfortunately, I have to talk to you about what, of course,
you will not like to hear. Don't be alarmed; I will be a
disciplined patient. From the analyses which Teresa made,
seeing me always tired, it turned out that the doctors
confirmed I am suffering from nephritis. The doctor hopes
that it is not chronic but simply an acute period. For the
record: I'm starving! The Doctor issued a letter to the
school, so I will have the month off. Time to heal the body
and the spirit.

One month later, Francesco shared some good news.

Legnano, 15 February 1932

Finally, some good news, thank goodness, but I don't think
I won the lottery. Yes, I believe I have healed my wounds
and would like to come to visit you by car.

But I forgot the best, Eureka! This morning, re-doing my
analysis, they found very little, barely perceptible albumin.
I've been in bed for two days continuously in warmth, not
working at all. Don't you think it's good news?

Sending a kiss to you. Stay healthy, and love each other
always.

Just one week later:

Legnano, 23 February 1932

Caro Peppino,
I am Lazarus: pains, insomnia, cravings, and no appetite.
I'm tired; I can't go on with my writing. I'm no longer
good for anything.

Legnano, 13 June 1932

Dear children,
I take the pen and write to you; the state where I find myself
is not easy. I have no strength left, I can't stand up, and
eating makes me sick. The other day I was so discouraged
that I reminisced about my beautiful and especially loving
one to me, my mother; I had a strong cry.

Legnano, 18 July 1932

Beloved children,
We are still in Legnano, not out of fear of time, not out of ill
will, but because the doctor's prodigies did not answer the
purpose. I'm a rag; I'm not hungry. Even when the weather
is good, I stay in bed or sit on the deck chair instead of
going for a walk. Free me from this state of affairs; I will
not bother you much longer. I need a fresh breath of air;
otherwise, I'll go to the cemetery to change the air.

Peppino's journal entry on 20 July 1932, states:

Papa's health had deteriorated considerably, so much so that it
was no longer easy for him to move without the help of a walking
stick, dragging himself with incredible difficulty. Nonetheless,
he wanted to perform his managerial duties fully. He writes,

"I plan to attend the student's final exams, addressing each to offer my good words, and wise advice; I want to preside over all the exams and rule in the administrative matters which is carried out between the offices of the Municipality and the college of teachers. That requires considerable effort from me, but, unfortunately, I do not think it is possible."

Peppino understood he needed to see his beloved father immediately, hoping his arrival would help lift Francesco's spirits. Upon his arrival, Francesco's mood moved from a person with little energy to one of genuine affection. He benefitted greatly at the sight of Peppino. Francesco said, "I feel I re-established my serene and most carefree good mood."

Peppino's 20 July journal entry continued later that day:

The magnificent walk along Simplon Road that runs along Lake Maggiore presented itself as one of the best aspects for Papa as he was able to enjoy it fully. With his youthful kindness and the various beauties of the enchanting panorama, he was content.

This was a day in Francesco's life that brought him his final happy moments.

Peppino reflected in his journal:

The next day, Papa remained in bed, without strength, completely motionless. His voice, once so sweet and strong, was now completely gone. My poor sick father could express his wishes only with hand gestures.

He began conducting the unforgettable memories which were undoubtedly in his head. For him, I am sure they were German symphony orchestras. His hands helped shape the expression on his face. To the hundred instrumentalists he had under him, the features of a performance [was] modeled according to his artistic sensibility. His hands laboriously waved above his head, but soon, falling dead weight on the bed, [they] expressed the impossibility of creating again the life that fatally abandoned him.

The change of air could not change an illness already too advanced to resolve itself with recovery. Francesco resisted another ten days until the dawn of 31 July 1932. Following internal bleeding, with a heavenly smile that strangely lit up his face, in the arms of his dear son Peppino and of his wife, he serenely returned his beautiful soul to God.

At the same time Francesco was dying, in the small convent on Lake Maggiore, pious Benedictine Sisters sang. At the break of dawn, they sang Francesco's *Ave Maria*. His music not only filled the air but his dying ears.

Legnano Bust

> "To be rooted is perhaps the most important and
> least recognized need of the human soul."
> –Simone Weil

I googled every permutation I could think of using our family name. From "Neglia music," to "Neglia composer," and from "Neglia artist," to "Neglia Enna," I covered dozens of possibilities. I was very happy to discover that the Neglia name, and my great-uncle's legacy lives on.

Each search took me down a new avenue of discovery. Most led me to Italian websites, others to those that accommodate Italian and English languages alike. I joined a group called "Neglia's del Mondo," or Neglias of the world, on a social media outlet. Once on the page, it wasn't hard to notice that the members, the vast majority of the Neglias, are in the arts. We have dancers, singers, actors, and instrumentalists who make up the vast majority of the membership. Is it a coincidence that the Neglia name is synonymous with the arts? I think not.

I am not suggesting that our family name carries the magical power of turning all into artists, but I was caught off guard by the sheer number of members who were tied to the arts.

In 1962, the municipality of Enna wanted to recognize their composer, Francesco Paolo, with a commemorative international competition for pianists and opera singers. This competition was an annual event for several years. After a hiatus, the 34th edition of the International Competition was scheduled to resume in 2020 but was postponed due to COVID-19.

Due to COVID-19, the 34th edition of the competition
was postponed to the summer of 2021

Its resumption is a milestone in the history of the city of Enna,
one which, by giving new life to a competition that was in danger of
disappearing, confirms its dedication to classical music.

I learned that there were several schools in Sicily in the name of
Francesco Paolo. The one pictured below is in the heart of Enna.

A school named after my Great Uncle, in Enna, Sicily

Among other exciting finds were streets named after him. Vie Francesco Paolo Neglia are located all over Sicily, and Italy, most notably in Enna, Rome, and Legnano. I also came across a piazza in Enna, directly outside The Church of San Tomasso. I typed the name of the church into the Wikipedia search bar and hit enter. Wikipedia states, in part: "The church of *San Tommaso,* which overlooks Piazza Francesco Paolo Neglia, boasts a 15th-century belfry with three orders. It has windows framed by an agile full-centered archivolt. The church contains a marble icon (1515) attributed to Giuliano Mancino and precious frescoes by Borremans."

Among the most beautiful squares along via Roma (in Enna) is one named after one of the most famous Sicilian musicians: Francesco Paolo Neglia.

Chiesa di Saint Tommaso, Enna, Sicily

As I look at the photographs and read the articles on my family, I do so with great pride, pride in our family name, profession, and life mission.

I am proud to have discovered this wonderful piazza, these street names, and schools, knowing the Neglia name will live on past my years and for all generations to come.

Piazza Francesco Paolo Neglia, Enna, Sicily

NIMROD

"One does not remember one's own pain. It is the suffering of others that undoes us." –Anna Funder

I have been in this business for decades now and have never feared whatever tasks were before me. The mountain of work that was on my lap seemed insurmountable, however. Before leaving for Jacksonville, but after accepting the position, I began to form a plan to put things in place. Not knowing what was waiting for me, I based my plan on past experiences.

That plan began with answering all the unanswered emails in the generic personnel manager's email box. When I signed in for the first time, I was astounded at the amount waiting for me. There were more than 180 unattended emails, mostly from musicians with various requests and needs.

I spent my first few days in Jacksonville reading and digesting the collective bargaining agreement, so when I responded to a request or demand, I knew that my response would follow the letter of the agreement. Sifting through emails, trying to understand who was who in the orchestra and what instrument they played proved to be a daunting task. How can I respond to their emails without knowing who I was speaking to? It was incredibly frustrating.

I would find myself referring to the Jacksonville Symphony website to confirm who people were. I worked diligently, methodically, and with complete focus. I worked devilishly hard, learning everyone's name and position, and committed their names and faces to memory. When I responded to each email, I would have an added level of assuredness for my files and wellbeing. Somewhere buried in the emails was one from a core member of the orchestra. Colin, a violist, was inquiring about returning to work.

Without any knowledge of why he was on sick leave, I wasn't able to answer him. I jotted an email to my general manager and soon learned that Colin had been placed on sick leave due to cancer complications.

I have dealt with friends, colleagues, and orchestra members succumbing to this dreaded disease during my career. Each time, experiencing this reality, I felt nothing but complete and utter heartbreak. I witnessed a light go out, the worst thing I can digest. The loss is unthinkable and devastating, the total collapse of a living being called to rest through the ultimate sacrifice.

In 2004, I had a close friend, one of five sisters, who died due to the unthinkable breast cancer. I loved her and was devoted to her well-being, her health, and her recovery.

A few months before her passing, she emailed and then called me to share that she was ready to come back to work. She was a member of the orchestra and had been out on sick leave for nearly a year. I shared that her seat was waiting and that none of her colleagues were nearly capable of filling her vacancy.

She laughed at me and proposed her return-to-work date. She was a genuinely inspirational person in every sense of the word: her depth, understanding, caring, and compassion transcended time and her sickness. As I write, I am tearing up at her glorious memory.

My friend had four sisters, one of whom married the twin brother of her spouse. It wasn't until much later that I learned that both sisters chose not to have children so they could cut off the cancer gene that had infected past and now current generations. At that time, I had no idea whatsoever that her sister was equally ill as she.

As a personnel manager, my entire life is all about taking notes of each day's events. But this is the first time I have ever discussed my relationship with the sisters. It was an extremely tough time for me, and I made a conscious decision not to document them or this story. Now, I feel compelled.

The pain I feel to this day, 5 January 2021, mimics the pain I suffered at the hands of time. When my friend contacted me about returning to work, I jumped for joy. We spoke of logistics and confidentiality. We also discussed that her doctor needed to write a release letter, allowing her to return to work.

In our organization, there is an excellent mechanism in place called "work hardening." Work hardening means I can bring a musician back slowly, perhaps have them play just the first half of a program, not the entire show. I could repeat this for several weeks or as needed. Joining the orchestra a little at a time would allow the returning musician to become acclimated to orchestra life—a perfect solution.

My beautiful friend refused any special accommodations and told me, "I am ready to reenter the workforce, fully and completely." Of course, I granted her request and set the wheels in motion. Upon her arrival, she performed at the expected level and with a smile beaming from a soul that exudes all that is good, true, and sincere. She was able to perform for the next few weeks without interruption. On one occasion, during a lunch break between services, she sat down next to me to eat her well-deserved meal. Although she sat to my right, we didn't speak much; we made constant peripheral eye contact, however. She was baiting me, with her warm smile, to discuss my latest and most exciting news with her, that of my relationship with my then-girlfriend, Sasha. My friend and Sasha were not only colleagues in the orchestra but performed regularly in a string quartet.

Unable to engage in a personal conversation, I shared acknowledging glances and heartfelt warmth for her support. At one point, while my hands were below the table surface, she grabbed my right hand and began to squeeze it in support of my love (although at that time hidden relationship) for my wife-to-be.

A few uneventful weeks passed, and all was well until I received a call that my friend was not feeling well. This call came from her sister; I took notice and concern. Because my friend was so private about her condition, I was hesitant to reach out to her. Instead, I reached out to the sister who contacted me.

A series of emails flurried back and forth; I learned my friend was not doing well and that there was no return-to-work date in the future. Imagine you just learned this news. Devastating to digest, process, and understand. Clutching my hands together, I kept repeating, please, help her.

I kept reaching out to my friend's sister. I needed information, news, any update from my ailing friend and colleague. Seeking out news was a horrible task for me, one I was unsure how to navigate. I had lived through a lot in life, but not this; not loving someone I felt might leave us soon. I felt her slipping away, and I was helpless to do anything. I wanted to share my concern; I wanted to let her know how much I cared about her and how much I wanted to help. I kept in touch with my friend's sister. Any news would be most welcome, but none followed.

Time passed slowly. Then, the most challenging part to recall took place. The sister of the friend stopped responding to my emails. There was no more contact, no more news, not one update, not a single word. What was happening? A few days later, I learned that the sister passed away from breast cancer. What am I hearing? In all the phone calls I shared with the sister, I had no idea that she was also sick. I was inconsolable.

I could share many stories about my relationship with my ailing friend, her sister, and their father. These relationships are even, to this day, painful to recount. We were all part of the same musical family; we had all worked together for years, both at the symphony and at freelance gigs; now, the unimaginable.

More sadness followed just a few weeks later. After losing my friend's sister, we lost my friend; both died due to breast cancer. I was overwhelmed with emotion, not for the moment, but, it felt, for life. My emotions pushed past my selfishness and landed on those of their parents and the twin brothers who were their husbands. The two sisters had died within weeks of each other. Their passing was only a year after the first sister passed due to the same ailment. Being a father myself, I cannot imagine losing a child, never mind three.

I suffered a horrible period in my personal life, one that, only now, 17 years later, I can share. How was it that a personnel manager can become so entangled with the membership that he could suffer as one with them? I have no answer, just knowledge.

Unfortunately, a similar emotion showered over me during my first months with the Jacksonville Symphony.

Colin contacted me about healthcare issues and about returning to work. I did everything I could to help put things in place for him to receive full benefits from the symphony.

I kept thinking about my friends who left us; Colin's sickness was real. I helped him through the process of returning to work. He had been out for an extended period before my joining as the personnel manager.

Ultimately, we did bring him back, and the personality behind all the emails became real to me when Colin entered the personnel office. He came to welcome me to the job and offer thanks for my help in bringing him back smoothly. Upon entering my office, I recall wishing to embrace him. I was so impressed with Colin, his desire to return to work, and his understanding of my position. Moreover, his drive and determination to return to the swing of things stood out above all others.

I shared with the membership and the staff that our family member was returning to work. All were appreciative of the welcome news.

Colin returned in December 2018; my first few months as the interim personnel manager were filled with many issues but not of this magnitude. Colin's situation offered me a greater realization of my continued desire to administer to others.

Of course, I welcomed him back with open arms, as did his colleagues on stage.

A few days before the New Year, he called me to share that he wasn't feeling well. He said that he was nauseous most of the time but thought it could be the lingering chemotherapy effects. A few days later, I called him just to check in, to ask how he was feeling. He informed me the doctors found a large mass in his stomach. I did my best to be supportive and speak words of encouragement, but I felt sick to my stomach as I hung up the phone.

I learned of his passing just a few weeks later; I tell you, the news horribly triggered the inner, most sensitive place within me. I suffered a blow that reminded me of my friend and her sister's passing a few years ago. The impact was direct and excruciating.

Upon his passing, a remarkable event occurred. The Jacksonville Symphony members banded together and began to put forth a plan. A memorial service was announced.

When the day of the memorial came, I attended. I found a seat in the church toward the back of the congregation, as I didn't want to take a closer seat. I felt those seats should be for his family and closest friends.

The musicians of the symphony attended in full force. Chamber groups would take place in the center of the sanctuary to perform selections of music between scripture readings.

It was impossible not to feel showered by the tenderness of the service, the praise of the spoken words, and the joyous sounds of the music offered to our fallen friend. Towards the end of the service, I witnessed one of the most remarkable moments I have seen in my life to date. Shortly after the pastor of the church completed his remarks, 40-45 people stood up. Those who stood were all members of the Jacksonville Symphony. They claimed the sanctuary, and within minutes transformed it into a makeshift concert hall stage. The orchestra members were to offer their honor to Colin through their performance.

A fellow member of the viola section, Jorge Peña, did not take his viola to play; no, he took the podium to lead the orchestra. Being a newcomer to the symphony, I didn't know of any other abilities of our musicians. Seeing Jorge with a baton in his hand intrigued me. What were they going to perform? What work was a worthy send-off to our colleague?

As they began, I knew from the first note that the selection they were performing was from the British composer Edward Elgar. They chose to extract a movement from the ever-popular *Enigma Variations*. *Enigma Variations* is perhaps Elgar's most famous work, one which I have performed at least two dozen times during my playing career.

The Variations are just that, a number of variations on a theme. The name of the ninth variation is "Nimrod." This variation has become popular in its own right and is sometimes used at British funerals, memorial services, and other solemn occasions. It is a beautifully lush, sweeping four minutes of music.

Jorge began by ever so slowly motioning his hands. The music started, and my heart began to sink further into my chest. Colin, my friend, her sister, and others became present at the moment. Adding to my heightened emotion, I watched the orchestra members, who came out in full force, perform so beautifully for our colleague.

My thoughts and emotions were alive, and I felt completely overwhelmed with my surroundings and thoughts. This glorious music was slowly enveloping the congregation. The pews were arranged in a semicircle, in the church. In the center was a large blow-up photograph of Colin, which sat on an easel for all to see.

The music began, slowly, ever so slowly to build. As the musical tension was building, so were my inner tensions; as the music was coming to its peak, I was approaching my emotional peak.

I was experiencing a sadness that I had experienced only once before with the passing of my 47-year-old brother. The sadness of his death overcame me. I could no longer hold back my emotion any longer. I could not grab a breath to help suppress what I knew I could not fight. I felt the hairs on my legs, chest, and arms tingle—my senses had never been more alive. It was then I burst into uncontrollable tears. Those who were sitting around me took notice; they were strangers, not knowing who I was.

I sat, consumed with the devotion of my colleagues' performance and Jorge's careful attention in his direction. It was a remarkable moment in my life. As I had never documented my friend's passing in New Jersey, this is the first time I have written anything on our colleague's passing in Jacksonville.

When the music concluded, I wish I could say that my tears subsided, but they didn't. After the pastor offered his final prayers and the service ended, I was met by all those sitting around me. They were all offering their condolences for the loss of what they thought was my best friend.

On my silent drive back to the hall, I had the thought that Colin represents everyone I had known who left us, old and young, family and friends. Colin represents the world at large, the suffering of the masses, the calling for peace, and the need to be grounded.

I have seldom experienced the intertwining of love and compassion with music, which heightened my state to join them as one. I was truly overwhelmed and never made it back to work. Instead, I went home to spend some quiet time reflecting on the meaning of life and how I fit in.

I share these two stories to help better understand myself, to better understand who I am, how I wish to live my life, and how I choose those around me. I share the memories of those who have done nothing wrong but have been dealt a hand that they could not control. They were all stronger than I can hope to be in life. I admire not just their desire to continue but their commitment. In their passing, I can only hope that they are able to feel the love and warmth of those they left behind.

SIBLINGS

"Invisible threads are the strongest ties" –Friedrich Nietzsche

Joe, Jim, John –circa 1967

40 years later, John, Joe, Jim –30 December 2007

Dorothy, Joe, Rossana —circa 1959

Dorothy, Rossana, Joe —circa 1961

L-R: Joe, Rossana, Dorothy, John, Jim –1964

front row, l-r: Jim, Rossana, John
back row: Joe and Dorothy –1966

I imagine those of us who are the youngest of siblings feel that we needed to speak and act louder, more aggressively than our older brothers and sisters. Well, if not, I certainly did. There were five of us siblings at the dinner table, five vying for our mother's attention, five in line to practice piano. Knowing there were four ahead of me was, itself, enough to lead to my absolute determination to push harder and excel in all I pursued. I had to surpass all expectations just to maintain my place at the bottom. My goal was to push even harder, so I could at least feel like I had a chance.

And why wouldn't I feel this way? Above me are four immensely talented brothers and sisters, each a ball of natural talent passed down from generations of musicians. In turn, my brother and sisters passed their abilities to their children, and now their children have another generation of musical, artistic offspring.

In my opinion, there is no coincidence at all. Our genes are all connected to Domenico, our great-great-grandfather from the early 19th century who was himself an accomplished musician.

Joe, Dorothy, Rossana, and John carried the family talent, each displaying an inherent ability to perform at extremely high levels. All are organists and singers who found much of their musical outlet in the church. Our father enjoyed a career in liturgical music, which was passed down to his children, grandchildren, and now, great-grandchildren.

At Saint Joseph's parish in Jersey City, my father began liturgical his career in 1967. Years later, when our father moved to another parish, Joe took over his vacant position. As the years progressed, and when Joe moved to another parish, Dorothy took over. History kept repeating itself, and when Dorothy accepted a job in another parish, Rossana began her tenure as the music director. Some thirty or so years after our father had stepped down, my brother John was now in his seat. In the winter of 1983, I joined John as leader of song and remained in that position until 1 January 2000. My performance career had taken off by then, and I could no longer balance out my duties in the church and concert hall.

As time passed, it was Dorothy's daughters who would move into my vacated position, and following my nieces, Rossana's son, my godson, took over. Thus, our family has been musicians at Saint Joseph's for the past 54 years. I am not surprised one bit by this; in fact, it seems to be as normal as breathing in and out. The music gene lives in all of us.

In the early days, when we were all living under the same roof, we would spontaneously gather in the music room to entertain ourselves. The music room contained a Yamaha baby grand piano, a complete set of drums, amplifiers for bass and six-string guitars, an autoharp, and a treasure trove of handheld percussion instruments. We had everything from tambourines and triangles, to rhythm sticks, maracas, guiro, djembe, frame drums, and a box filled with sound effects.

Sitting to the right of the piano was a vast array of songbooks. We had everything from Sinatra; Crosby, Stills & Nash; The Beatles; the best of Neapolitan music; and other popular songbooks. We would gather around and just start flipping through the books, singing, playing, and enjoying each other. These memories are among the happiest times of my early years.

It was very common on most songs for my siblings to break into three- and four-part harmony, none of which are written in the books! They just sang what they heard in their heads. The music was pure, unforced, and everyone knew what to play or sing without direction. Yes, we were all in each other's heads, hearts, and music. Hours would pass before we felt it was time to wrap things up.

I was, and still am, in awe of my siblings; there is so much talent ingrained in them. Although I felt smothered by their overwhelming talents, I pressed on in the hope of keeping up with them. Digging deeper and deeper into my inner abilities, I felt the need to push myself further. It wasn't their fault they were born with so much talent, but at times, it felt that the gene pool lessened by the time I was born. Of course, that isn't true, but at the time, it certainly felt so.

They are all giants in my eyes, and all I wanted to do was live up to their level and expectations. I wanted to have my voice heard just as my siblings had in such an unforced way.

Decades later, I still see each of them as miracles. They have harnessed the power of music and, to this day, share it with so many others. Whether they are ministers of music, music therapists, or music educators, the Neglia family has spent our entire lives ministering to others. Sharing our gifts with congregations at weddings, we share healing music at funerals and music to celebrate each week's liturgy. We minister to those who hunger and yearn for the healing sounds of music from the hospital room, care centers, and performance halls throughout the world.

It is said that music heals all, and in my mid- to later years, I can honestly say that the gift of giving is one of the most beautiful offerings we are blessed to share. Living an altruistic life, one where caring and sharing leads to immeasurable happiness, only became possible due to my life in music. It is music that is the staple of our people, our parents, grandparents, and in my case, all past generations.

I have worked extremely hard on honing my skills, so much so that I finally feel I do have a voice in our musical family. It has been my joy to maintain and contribute to my place in the family tradition. Together, with my siblings, nieces, and nephews, we jointly move our family lineage from generation to generation.

Back row, l-r: my father, Joseph; grandfather, Angelo;
brothers Joe and John and sister Rossana.
Front row: Maria, my mother; Vina, holding me in her arms;
my father's mother, Dora; and Dorothy in the front
—1964

Researching my past has been a blessing in so many ways—not only because I can preserve and share my findings, but also because I have, for the first time, a knowledge of my family's earliest recorded focus in music.

With this new knowledge, I can see exactly how I fit into our family history and how the Neglia DNA has passed from Domenico to current generations. Thinking specifically of my family tree, I fully support the studies that suggest that talent is passed down through our bloodline.

MOMENTS IN TIME

"You only grow by coming to the end of something
and by beginning something else." –John Irving

Choosing the photographs to share within the covers of this book proved to be a difficult process. As I was sorting, purging, I caught myself hesitating more times than not. I decided, instead of omitting the photographs that were under consideration, I would add them in their own chapter, as a sort of epilogue.

The picture here is the inaugural concert of the Music Hall in Hamburg. I love this photograph as the perspective of the audience is from the timpani position. I spent over 35 years in that exact position. The view from that vantage point is and will forever be emblazoned in my memory.
photo credit: Mario Barbieri, *FP Neglia, La Vita Le Opera*

The plaque sits on the façade of the birthplace
of my great uncle, Francesco Paolo.
Location: Via Paolo Vetri, Enna, Sicily

The Plaques reads:
Francesco Paolo Neglia
glorious musician of Italy
was born in this house
Returning from triumphs in foreign lands
the most intense years of his life
his spirit, troubled by the adversity of fate
found comfort from the peace of his memory

The City of Enna
thirty years after his death
honors the great son in this marble
by inscribing his name among
the major pioneers
of the Italian Symphony
A permanent record for future generations
XXXI. VII. MCMLXII

Francesco Paolo in Legnano. This is the last known
photograph of my great uncle known to me.

Maria posing for the Fly National, "Airline of
the Stars" promotion —circa 1954

Emma and Peppino —circa 1909

Caricature of Master Liborio Neglia
by one of his pupils
photo credit: Laura Fusaro, *Maestro sul podio e nella vita*

Apple TV opening with Sasha and our friends —October 2019

My brother John and me at a monument to our great uncle in Enna, Sicily. This photograph represents the only time John and I were in Sicily together. —1986

Not only did we inherit musical abilities from our father's side, but our mother, Vina, was an artist. John, who was a gifted artist, would constantly doodle. In one of his notepads, I found three different pictures to share. Although they were obviously penned quickly, the three display John's thinking of musicians in an orchestral setting. (1) A timpanist who inadvertently uses a chicken drumstick as a mallet. (2) A violin and flute duo, where the flutist becomes exposed as the wearer of a hairpiece. (3) A caricature of a busy, and then exhausted conductor. I chose the last picture because I feel it represents generations of Neglia music making. Many of our ancestors sat under the baton of such a conductor. See the back cover for this little gem from my brother.

Lickin-Chicken by John Neglia —1988

Toupée by John Neglia –1988

Neglia Conservatorium: violin lesson
This photo reminds me of my days studying at the Mannes
College of Music. I recall seeing a very similar picture
in David Mannes' memoir, *Music is my Faith*.
photo credit: Mario Barbieri, *FP Neglia, La Vita Le Opera*

Performing (I am on the right) in Cuenca, Spain –July 2005

All five of us grew up singing in our church choir. This photograph
was captured when I was eight years old. The photo was taken
at Saint Michael's Monastery, Union City, New Jersey –1971
Front row: I am pictured 2nd from the left, and my brother John is
on the far right in the same row. In the back row, on the left, is our
father, Joseph, and second from the right is my older brother, Joe.

My Great Grandfather, Giuseppe, with his
grandchildren Peppino and Emma —1909
photo credit *Mario Barbieri, La Vita Le Opera*

My sister, Dorothy, our Aunt Maria, and my
brother Joe —circa 1972

FP conducts at an inauguration of a Monument –circa 1930
photo credit: Laura Fusaro, *Maestro sul podio e nella vita*

Joseph and Maria playing together –circa 1938

Maria and her brother, Joseph, in NYC –1951

John at the Piano –2009

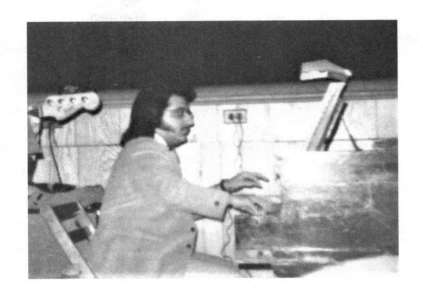

Joe at the piano –circa 1973

John and Jim –1965

Princeton, New Jersey –July 2017

My father, Joseph, and mother, Vina, with Joe and Dorothy
–circa 1956

Completing this book has proven to be one of my greatest accomplishments, not only for writing my fourth book but for the topics covered within the pages of this offering. I hope I have created an unmistakable footprint of the Neglia family and how we are all tied together through our common traits.

The Neglia name shall live on, not only through monuments, street names, and schools but through our heritage and commitment to the performing arts. I can recognize the countless performances of our past and present generations, of which the numbers are vast.

When I began this writing project, it was to learn and share as much information on our family as I could unearth. Once completed, the book took on a new meaning. With this publication, future generations will not have to translate books from one language to another or spend countless hours researching every detail of our past. I have done the work and share the results, knowing that our future generations will have to refer only to this book to understand the inner dynamics of the Neglia family. Our name shall live on in future generations, both on and off the stage.

Joe, Dorothy, Rossana, and myself, West Orange, New Jersey –29 August 2021

I am a proud member of the family who shares the name Neglia. Let the music and heritage live on for all future generations to reflect, enjoy, and join their earlier ancestors' mission. We welcome you!

Il nostro nome di famiglia continua a vivere—our family name lives on!

APPENDIX I - THE NEGLIA FAMILY TREE

"Since he was a boy, Neglia was attentive to the musical climate that surrounded him. After all, he was born into a family that made music for several generations and had breathed music from the earliest cries." –Maurizio Agrò

Familienname	Vorname	Geburts-datum und -ort	Ge-schlecht m. | w.	Art der Urkunde	Daten d Ausstellung d Urkunden	von wem ausgestellt bzw. geführt? (Staatsanwalt? Gericht? Polizei? Rechtsanwalt? Finanzamt etc.?)	Aufbewahrungsort der Originalurkunde
1	2	3	4	5	6	7	8
Natile	Franceako	17.10.22 Putignano	m	Aufenth. Anzeige	23.5.39	Polizei	Polizei
Nava	Tomaso	3.3.08 Cannero	m		29.1.40	"	"
Neglia	Angelo	9.1.86 Enna	m		1.6.44	"	"
Neglia	Giuseppe	3.3.29 Triest	m		1.7.44	"	"
Neglia	Maria	7.5.27 Triest	w		1.7.44	"	"

Judicial record from Europe, Registration of Foreigners and German Persecutees, Wiesbaden, Germany –1939-1947

Domenico Neglia born circa 1810 married Anna Liuzzo had one son:

Giuseppe 18 March 1846 † 17 September 1914
 m. Maria Greca. They had six children:
1. Lucia 13 December 1872 † 5 November 1949
2. **Francesco Paolo** 22 May 1874 † 31 July 1932
 First wife, Maria Dibbern 13 Sept 1877 † 29 January 1923
  Emma 2 October 1902 † 1957
  Giuseppe Adolfo (Peppino) 13 Mar 1904 † 19 Oct 1974
   m. Barbara Massimilla Daverio
    Giuseppina (b. 16 December 1933)
     m. Roberto Lelli
      Luisa, (b. 11 Sept 1962)
  Jolanda Beatrice 9 December 1917 † 2013
   Maria (b. 12 June 1943)
 Second wife Teresa Rotharmel
  Francesco Fortunato 11 November 1924 † 23 July 2003

3. Liborio 22 April 1876 † 24 August 1943
 m. Maria Leonardi
  Maria Evelina 11 February 1913 † 5 March 1988
   m. Eider Ravinale
    Fiammetta 20 September 1950
    Paolo 20 June 1961
  Elena 20 November 1922 † 4 December 2013
   m. Bonfiglio (dates unknown)
    Lucia (b. 2 September 1944)
     m. Giuseppe Agrò
      Maurizio (b. 10 Feb 1977)
      Tiziana (b. 27 April 1981)
    Maria Catania (b. 11 February 1946)
     m. Paternico
      Antonio (b. 16 February 1975)
      Viviana (b. 26 February 1983)
    Patrizia Catania (b. 6 October 1963)
     m. Pasqua (dates unknown)
      Fabio Torino (b. 17 Dec 1991)

4. Clementina 29 November 1880 † 21 September 1918

5. Angelo (my grandfather) 11 January 1886 † 5 May 1967
   First wife, Bice Vicini (dates unknown)
       Amalia (dates unknown)
       m. Piana (dates unknown)
           Giulia (b. 15 November 2004)
       Nennella (dates unknown)

   Second wife, Dora Biondi 22 Dec 1904 † 10 August 1996
       Maria 7 August 1927 † 27 August 2016
       Giuseppe (my father) 3 March 1929 † 12 May 2014

   Giuseppe's first wife, Vina Maria Profita 29 May 1930 † 16 January 1998
   They had five children:

       Joseph 2 September 1952
           m. Theresa Reynolds (b. 3 July 1954)
               Joseph Michael, 27 March 1985
               Michael Edward, 17 October 1987
                   m. Katherine Colmerauer (b. 18 Dec 1986)
                   Arlo 4 April 2018

       Dorothy 6 December 1955
           m. Joseph Sgalia (18 December 1954 † 21 April 2018)
               Gina Michele 17 April 1983
               m. Martin Ball, Jr. (b. 4 March 1967)
                   Vincent 15 August 2008
                   Nicholas 4 March 2012
               Laura Jean 19 March 1987
                   m. Victor Jose Muniz (b. 8 November 1985)
                   Luca Joseph 2 September 2020

Rossana 29 November 1958
    m. Nicholas Picini (b. 26 March 1959)
        John, 18 April 1986
            m. Sophia Crocetti (b. 25 December 1991)
    m. Robert McLaughlin (b. 24 January 1964)
        Alessano 18 August 2000

John 25 September 1962 † 10 January 2010
    m. Diane Costantino (b. 23 May 1960)

James 24 October 1963
    m. Alexandra Gorokhovsky (b. 6 November 1969)
        Phillip 28 September 1993
            m. Zoë Wasserman (b. 24 April 1994)
        Daniel 28 April 2004

Giuseppe's second wife, Lisa Picone (b. 2 May 1961)
They had three children:

    Dina 17 June 1985
        m. Grigor Khachatryan (b. 19 December 1986)
           Julietta Adriana 11 March 2016
           Ariana Chiara 8 June 2018
           Leo Vincenzo 7 May 2021
    Michael 29 August 1986
    Anthony 20 July 1989

6.   Giovanni 6 March 1896 † 9 January 1914

APPENDIX II

<u>JACKSONVILLE SAFETY PROTOCOL FOR COVID-19</u>

In collaboration with the Orchestra Committee, AFM Local 444, and IATSE Local 115, we have produced the following guidelines to ensure a safe and comfortable return to work for all.

We recommend that all personnel strictly observe safety precautions set forth by the CDC, in addition to the procedures outlined in this document pertaining to operations within the Times-Union Center for the Performing Arts. While we cannot enforce certain behaviors outside of the workplace, we strongly encourage all employees of the Jacksonville Symphony and all employees working in Jacoby Hall to engage in social distancing at all times. Any risky behavior puts the health of colleagues and the whole Symphony in jeopardy. Musicians who do not live in the same household are strongly encouraged to maintain social distancing (masks, 6 feet of distance) from the time they exit their car until they return to it after work.

Musicians that fall in the definition of "People at Increased Risk for Severe Illness" as defined by the CDC, or who share a household with someone that fits the definition, will not be required to perform live with other Musicians but may be required to provide mutually agreed alternative services for the JSA. The JSA may require a letter from the Musician's physician confirming that the Musician (or member of the Musician's household) falls within the definition of "People at Increased Risk for Severe Illness."

We strongly recommend that all orchestra members and employees take a diagnostic COVID-19 test before returning to work. Please reference the Florida Department of Health COVID-19 testing website for locations and additional information. We have received reports that the Regency Square testing site is particularly efficient.

The personnel manager will provide this safety plan to all non-member musicians performing with the orchestra. Those musicians will be required to follow all guidelines outlined in this document.

We will continually monitor and provide updates as safety and health recommendations develop. As the situation and science evolve, updates or revisions to this safety plan may periodically be provided to adhere to new guidelines. We understand that we will need to adjust or delay these plans should conditions demand it.

WHAT TO DO IF YOU FEEL SICK

Click here for the CDC's list of COVID-19 Symptoms. www.cdc.gov/coronavirus/symptoms

People with COVID-19 have experienced symptoms ranging from mild to severe illness. Symptoms may appear 2-14 days after exposure to the virus. People with these symptoms may have COVID-19:

- Fever or chills
- Cough
- Shortness of breath or difficulty breathing
- Fatigue
- Headache
- Muscle or body aches
- New loss of taste or smell
- Sore throat
- Congestion or runny nose
- Nausea or vomiting
- Diarrhea

DAILY SELF CHECK-UP

Answer YES or NO to the following questions:

Have you felt sick or had a fever of over 100.4 degrees in the past 24 hours?

Have you experienced any of the symptoms listed above in the past 24 hours?

If you answered YES to any of these questions, please seek medical attention immediately, and inform the personnel manager.

STEP BY STEP

Step by step process: Musician/Employee is symptomatic:

- Musician/Employee experiences symptoms and contacts their primary care provider or immediately goes in for a COVID-19 test.
- Musician/Employee is tested for COVID-19.
- Musician/Employee begins Isolation at home as soon as Musician experiences symptoms and until they receive test results.
- Musician/Employee notifies the Personnel Manager/Department head that they are sick and will be home. Musician/Employee is not required to provide the reason.
- Musician/Employee receives the COVID-19 test results.

If the test is negative:

- Musician/Employee leaves Isolation and returns to work if they are symptom-free. If the Musician/Employee is still experiencing symptoms, they should return to their provider for repeat evaluation.
- Musician/Employee emails Personnel Manager of returning to work.

If the test is positive:

- Musician/Employee notifies Personnel Manager/Department head.
- Contact tracing begins.
- People identified in contact tracing are notified by the Personnel Manager/Department head of a required 14-day quarantine.

On day 6 of Quarantine, it is recommended that the Musician/Employee be tested for COVID-19. If the test is positive, the Musician/Employee follows that process.

- After 14-days with no symptoms, Quarantine will end, and the Musician/Employee can return to work.
- If during Quarantine, they experience symptoms, they should follow the process above.
- After 10+ days in Isolation AND 72 hours without a fever (without a fever-reducing agent) AND symptoms have improved, the Musician may retest.
- If negative, the Musician/Employee will test again in 24+ hours. Once the Musician/Employee receives two negative test results, they will move out of isolation.
- Musician/Employees should email negative test results to the Personnel Manager/Department head.

Step by step process: Musician/Employee is asymptomatic COVID-19 positive:

- Musician/Employee is not under Quarantine and had a COVID-19 test performed without the presence of symptoms.
- Musician/Employee begins Isolation at home as soon as a positive test result is confirmed and begins monitoring for the development of symptoms.
- Musician/Employee notifies the Personnel Manager/Department head.
- Contact tracing begins.
- People identified in contact tracing are notified by the Personnel Manager of a required 14-day Quarantine.
- On day 6 of Quarantine, it is recommended that the Musician be tested for COVID-19. If the test is positive, the Musician/Employee follows that process.
- After 14 days with no symptoms, Quarantine will end, and the Musician/Employee can return to work.

- If during Quarantine, they experience symptoms, they should follow the process above.
- After 10+ days in Isolation AND no onset of symptoms, the Musician/Employee may retest.
- If negative, the Musician will test again in 24+ hours. Once the Musician receives two negative test results, they will move out of Isolation.
- Musician/Employees should email negative test results to the Personnel Manager/Department head.

Step by step process: Musician has been exposed to COVID-19:

- Musician/Employee learns their child, partner, spouse, close contact, et al., has tested positive for COVID-19.
- Musician/Employee notifies the Personnel Manager/ Department head of the required 14-day quarantine.
- A negative COVID-19 test during quarantine does not authorize the Musician/Employee to return to work.
- Musician/Employee begins 14-day quarantine at home.
- On day 6 of Quarantine, it is recommended that the Musician/ Employee be tested for COVID-19. If the test is positive, the Musician/Employee follows that process.
- After 14 days with no symptoms, the Musician/Employee can return to work.
- If the Musician/Employee develops symptoms, see the above process.
- Musician/Employee Isolation count begins the first day of onset symptoms.

Isolation vs. Quarantine:
- Isolation is used for someone who has COVID-19 symptoms or is positive for COVID-19
- Quarantine is used to separate someone who was possibly exposed to COVID-19 to determine if they develop symptoms.

Test-based strategy to return to work

- After 10+ days in Isolation AND 72 hours without a fever (without a fever-reducing agent) AND symptoms have improved, the Musician/Employee may retest.
- If negative, the Musician/Employee will test again in 24+ hours. Once the Musician/Employee receives two negative test results, they will move out of Isolation.
- Musician/Employees should send negative test results to the Personnel Manager/Department head.

SANITIZATION, SAFETY, and COMFORT

- All filters within the Jacoby Symphony Hall HVAC system are upgraded to MERV-13, a high-quality, high-efficiency filter.
- All restrooms will be sanitized daily.
- Drinking fountains throughout the Times-Union Center will be turned off.
- High touch areas throughout the backstage area will be sanitized daily.
- Hand sanitizer will be provided throughout the backstage and audience areas.

Floor-standing plexiglass shields will be placed in front of wind and brass musicians as well as in between wind and brass musicians as needed to protect against aerosol dispersal.

- Orchestra equipment on stage, such as music stands and plexiglass shields, will be sanitized daily by the stage crew. Strings will not be rotated between pieces so that one person sits in one chair the entire service. If chairs must be shared during a service, the stagehand must wear new gloves to move the chair and wipe it down before another musician may sit down or a new chair will be brought out.

- All instruments with a bell will use a fabric covering to reduce aerosol output. Those instruments will not be required to use a mute.
- Musicians whose instruments require emptying of condensation will use absorbing pads on the stage floor. Individual musicians will be required to change out their own pads following every service. Pads will be provided by the JSA. Please see the personnel manager.
- Until it is determined to be safe to hold longer rehearsals and concerts, rehearsals and concerts will not exceed 90 minutes.
- Due to the variability of conditions in Jacoby Hall and limited access to lockers, musicians are advised to arrive at services prepared with layers of clothing appropriate to the type of service.

FACE COVERINGS

- Masks must be worn at all times when inside the Times-Union Center, including in all common areas and throughout the backstage areas. This applies to all JSA and ASM employees, contractors, extra musicians and stage crew, and audiences.
- To the extent possible, wind and brass players are required to wear masks that can be worn while playing.
- All masks must be worn so that both mouth and nose are covered at all times, to the extent possible while playing.
- "Vented" and "valved" masks are not permitted.
- All masks worn for performances must be black. Masks worn for rehearsals may be any color.
- Flutes will be required to use wind defenders.
- Musician masks, wind defenders, and bell coverings are provided by AFM Local 444.

BUILDING ENTRY

- Your temperature will be taken upon entering the building. If your temperature is higher than 100.4 degrees, you will not be permitted entry, and you should contact the personnel manager/department head immediately.
- If arriving with others, stand at a proper distance of at least six feet while waiting for your temperature check.
- Floors throughout the backstage areas and the musicians' lounge will be marked with decals showing appropriate distancing. Please maintain a distance of at least six feet from other musicians using those markings.
- To the extent possible, doors will be propped open in order to facilitate touchless entry.
- Traffic patterns and one-way traffic markings will be placed on the floor throughout the backstage areas.
- Equipment will be removed from the backstage crossover to allow two-way traffic lanes with better spacing. Tables will be set up to facilitate unpacking areas for performances only.

MUSICIANS LOUNGE

- The chairs and tables along the windows will be removed for this season.
- The lounge kitchen area will not be available for use, and coffee will not be provided; however, the touch-less bottle filling station will be available.
- Congregating is strictly prohibited before or after services. Please plan to move quickly and efficiently through the musicians' lounge and any musician holding space.
- On double-service days, musicians will be required to leave the building between services.

The guest artist dressing rooms will not be available for practice, rehearsals, or as meeting space throughout the 20-21 season unless specifically arranged with Artistic Operations staff.

- Musician mailboxes will not be in use during the 20-21 season. Checks and any other documents normally distributed via mailboxes will be mailed to your address on file.
- The musicians' lounge bulletin board will not be in use during the 20-21 season. The personnel manager will communicate all material electronically.
- No guests will be permitted in the musicians' lounge, backstage, or any musician holding space. Please arrange to meet any guests outside the Times-Union Center.
- Access to lockers may be restricted throughout the season.

MUSICIAN HOLDING SPACES

- For rehearsal services, musicians will be assigned to use either the musicians' lounge or Jacoby Hall for uncasing and personal belongings. Entry procedures are outlined in detail in the REHEARSALS section. The personnel manager will communicate assignments.
- For concert services, musicians will be assigned to use either the musicians' lounge or the cross-over for uncasing and personal belongings. The personnel manager will communicate assignments.

RESTROOMS

- Before and after rehearsals, musicians who uncase instruments in Jacoby will have access to the lobby restrooms via the rear doors to the lobby.
- Musicians in the Musicians Lounge will use the lounge restrooms as normal.

- In all cases, every other stall will be available. Restrooms will be serviced regularly.

MUSIC AND LIBRARY

Library
- Entry to the library is strictly limited to librarians and select staff as needed.
- General library requests should be made at least 48 hours in advance by email to Bart Dunn.

Folder Procedures

- Folders will be cleaned before and after use for any given concert series.
- Library staff will wear latex gloves when assembling and disassembling folders.
- Folders will sit for a three-day period before and after distribution and return.
- One folder per player, as per usual concert distribution.
- Each string player will receive all bowed original parts.
- All part rotations for winds, brass, and percussion should be communicated to the library and personnel manager no later than 21 days before the start of any given concert set.
- Folder distribution will take place over a three-day period. Email notifications will be sent out as to which folders are available, when, and where. There will not be a sign-out sheet for the 20-21 season.
- Following performances, players should return their folders to the cart placed backstage. Folders may not be returned via any other means except with the express approval of the library.

Rehearsal and Performance Procedures
- Individual musicians will be responsible for carrying their folder(s) to and from the stage for both rehearsals and performances.

- Musicians will be responsible for moving their folders in the event of a stage set change.
- Requests for additional copies of music or other musical needs during rehearsals or performances can be made by email or phone call. The requested material will be left in the empty cart outside of the library door for the player to pick up.

REHEARSALS

- For rehearsal services, please enter the Times-Union Center as normal through the main security entrance.
- The stage will be available for warm-up 30 minutes before rehearsal start times.
- Please arrive at the Times-Union Center no earlier than 40 minutes before the rehearsal start time.
- Warm-up is permitted only on stage. No warm-up is allowed in the musician's lounge, any musician holding space other than Jacoby Hall, or any other space, including stairwells and Jacoby side hallways.
- Depending on the specific repertoire, durations of works, and stage configurations, musicians may be required to remain on stage for the duration of a service. This will be determined on a program-by-program basis.
- After the temperature check is complete, a selected number of musicians will proceed to the musicians' lounge. The personnel manager will communicate additional musician holding spaces as needed.
- All other members proceed directly into Jacoby Hall following the foot decals; do not enter the musicians' lounge.
- Once in Jacoby Hall, make your way directly to a designated instrument uncasing location.
- When you have uncased your instrument, proceed onto the stage via the house stage steps. Handrails will be added to stage steps.

- While proceeding to the stage, maintain an appropriate distance from other musicians.
- Once you have taken your place on stage, remain in your place for the duration of the service, do not move around the stage.
- To facilitate cleaning, take all personal items and your music folder with you when you leave the stage. No items may be left on stage following services.
- A sound reinforcement system will be in place on stage, and conductors will use a microphone to address the orchestra.

Exiting the Stage
- For all services, musicians will exit the stage in the following order:
- Strings starting from the back of each section
- Brass, Percussion, and Keyboard
- Woodwinds
- At all times, please maintain a minimum distance of six feet

CONCERTS
- For concert services, all musicians should enter the Times-Union Center via the musicians' lounge entrance. Your temperature will be taken, and you will be signed in.
- The stage will be available for warm-up 30 minutes before the concert start time.
- Please arrive at the Times-Union Center no earlier than 40 minutes before the concert start time.
- Warm-up is permitted only on stage. No warm-up is allowed in the musician's lounge, any musician holding space other than Jacoby Hall, or any other space, including stairwells and Jacoby side hallways.
- Depending on the specific repertoire, durations of works, and stage configurations, musicians may be required to remain on stage for the duration of a service. This will be determined on a program-by-program basis.

- The personnel manager will communicate musician holding areas other than the musicians' lounge before concerts.
- Musicians must arrive at the Times-Union Center in concert dress. No changing will be permitted in the building.
- After concerts, please leave the stage immediately. Congregating on stage or greeting guests in Jacoby Hall will not be permitted.
- To facilitate cleaning, take all personal items and your music folder with you when you leave the stage. No items may be left on stage following services.
- Due to the reduced capacity of Jacoby Hall and other venues, comp tickets will generally not be available during the 20-21 season. Comp tickets may be made available on a case-by-case basis.

INSTRUMENT CASES AND PERSONAL BELONGINGS

- In order to avoid trip hazards and facilitate safe and easy movement throughout the stage, our practices regarding instrument cases on stage remain in place.
- Wind players may bring cases on stage.
- All other musicians must leave cases in designated uncasing areas.
- No other personal belongings may be brought on stage.
- If any unlockable space within the Times-Union Center is used as a musician holding area, a guard will be provided to protect musicians' personal belongings.
- Musicians should bring their own cough drops as needed.
- Disposable earplugs will be available from the Personnel Manager.

EXTERNAL SERVICES, RUNOUTS, AND TOURS

Safety protocols for External Services, Runouts,[1] and Tours will be developed with the Travel Committee on a case-by-case basis.

---

1   Runouts are external services which last less than two days.

AUDIENCE SAFETY PROTOCOL

Parking

- Pre-purchased pass is good for the Pearl Street garage or the surface lot behind the Omni Hotel (entry on Bay Street).
- Garage has two-person or one-party limits in elevators, and stairwells are one-way.

Building Entry

- Masks are required to enter the Times-Union Center for the Performing Arts. Masks will be provided for those who do not have them, but we ask that you try to bring your own.
- Touchless temperature checks will be required before entry into the Times-Union Center for the Performing Arts.
- Lines to enter the building will be physically distanced as marked on the pavement.

Times-Union Center for the Performing Arts Lobby Protocols

- Masks must be worn at all times while in the Times-Union Center for the Performing Arts.
- Symphony concert start times have been moved to 7:30 PM
- Ticket takers will look at your tickets but will not take them from you or touch them.
- Hand sanitizer stations will be located throughout the lobby areas. Concessions and bars will be located near or in the Uible Gallery. Drinks and food will only be allowed in the Uible Gallery, where patrons can temporarily remove their masks. Masks must be worn outside the Uible Gallery.
- Restroom facilities will be reduced by 50%, thereby reducing the number of people in the restrooms at any given time. Lines for restroom facilities will be physically distanced as marked on floors.

- No more than four people will be allowed into the elevator at one time. In the case of a wheelchair, only two people will be permitted in the elevator.

Jacoby Symphony Hall Protocols

- Masks must be worn at all times in Jacoby Symphony Hall. Each patron will be assigned a specific door through which they will enter Jacoby Symphony Hall. Your door assignment will be the closest entry point to your seat location. This will reduce lines at the doors and in the aisles in the Hall.
- Jacoby Symphony Hall will be physically distanced with approximately 6' between groups of patrons. Boxes will not be physically distanced but will have plexiglass screens between patron groups. View Hall Map.
- Performances are expected to last between 60 and 75 minutes, and there will be no intermission.

Encore Magazine

Concert program information, including program notes, will be available digitally. We will also have a one-page hand-out available at the concert.

Times-Union Center for the Performing Arts Cleaning Protocols

- All high-touch areas, such as banisters, elevator buttons, seating, etc., in the lobby areas, will be thoroughly cleaned before each concert in the building.

Jacoby Symphony Hall Cleaning Protocols

- Every banister, seat armrest, door handle, and plexiglass screen will be thoroughly cleaned and sanitized after each concert.
- There are over 50 high-grade air filters in Jacoby Symphony Hall. They are checked and changed regularly.

Jacoby Symphony Hall Staff and Musicians

- All staff and musicians will have their temperature taken before entering the Times-Union Center for the Performing Arts.
- All staff members are required to wear masks.

Tickets

- For questions or concerns, please call the Box Office. We will continue to update the website if we receive additional information.

ACKNOWLEDGMENTS

Upon completing any project, no matter how small or large, along with a feeling of accomplishment, and satisfaction, I feel it is imperative to thank all those who supported me during my journey. Without them, I would be nowhere.

Support comes in many different forms: those who share historical information, discover anecdotes, share rarely-seen photographs, compare documents, capture art through the photo lens, design covers, and translate documents, to name a few.

My first line of support has consistently come from my wife, Sasha. Night after night, she would wake me up after I passed out at the computer keyboard, ensuring I got enough rest to start all over again in the morning. Thank you for helping me see this project from inception to completion.

I would like to recognize our sons, Phillip and Daniel, who have offered their opinions on how to proceed and their thoughts on the layout and formatting of the book. I am proud of our sons and the men they have become.

I am thrilled to acknowledge my friend and relative, Maurizio Agrò. I was able to translate his book from Italian to understand my great uncle's life better. Additionally, Maurizio was able to help fill in all those missing pieces of the Neglia puzzle I needed to complete this book. I am grateful to the photographs he shared, his written words, and his friendship.

Likewise, I am happy to share my gratitude for Laura Fusaro, who wrote the book, *Maestro, sul podio e nella vita*. Here I learned more information about my great uncle, but more exciting were some of the photographs I used in this book. It was Laura who shared with me photographs of my extended family. This was the first time I had ever set eyes on some of the family members. Before her publication, I never saw Liborio, Emma, or Maria Evelina.

My thanks to the Jacksonville Symphony Association for permission to reproduce the COVID-19 Safety Protocol document.

The dust cover design credit goes to Colleen K. Mallon. This is the third cover she has designed for me, and I know we will work together again on my next book. She also created the magnificent family tree illustration in the Neglia Family Tree section of the book. Her vision, talents, and remarkable creativity are an inspiration, and I am thrilled with her endless imagination.

A special thanks to the most exceptional copy and line editor in the industry, Eric B. Chernov. Eric is always pushing me to "think like a writer"—I am grateful!

With appreciation to all who assisted me on this journey.

-Jim Neglia

PHOTO CREDITS

All photographs in this book are owned by the
author except where otherwise credited.

My thanks to the following for graciously providing the
photographs in the book.

❖ Maurizio Agrò - from his book: *Francesco Paolo Neglia, Nella Vita e nell'arte*

❖ Laura Fusaro, from her book: *Maestro Sul Podio e nella Vita*

❖ Mario Barbieri, from his book: *FP Neglia, La Vita Le Opera*

❖ Steve Oroz/Michael Ochs "Toast of the Town" hosted by Ed Sullivan

ABOUT THE AUTHOR

Jim Neglia is a veteran force in the Performing Arts. He has been a working percussionist as well as an international music contractor and orchestra personnel manager for more than 35 years, working closely with some of the best-known names in the industry. From classical artists André Watts and Yo-Yo-Ma, to such contemporary artists as Huge Jackman and The Who, Neglia covers the entire gamut of music production and performance.

During his career, he performed with The New Jersey Symphony Orchestra, The New York City Opera, Ringling Brothers & Barnum and Bailey Circus, and performed live on the radio program *All Things Considered*. He has made various recordings for RCA, Decca, Albany, and Leonarda Records. Jim's career also took him abroad, working in 27 countries as a solo and orchestral percussionist. He has appeared and performed in the motion pictures *I love NY* with Christopher Plummer and *Joe Gould's Secret* with Stanley Tucci.

After writing his autobiographical books, *Onward and Upward* and *Center Stage*, Neglia took a break from writing about the on-stage portion of his life to concentrate on the off-stage, collector's side. During the pandemic of 2020, Neglia published *Visitors from the Past*, where he shares his collection of visiting cards of famous composers, conductors, and instrumentalists. Neglia's collection is the most extensive collection in the world.

Currently, Jim keeps a busy schedule as an orchestra personnel manager and international music coordinator. He resides in Florham Park, New Jersey, with his wife, Alexandra, and son, Daniel. For relaxation, he enjoys reading, writing, and collecting autographs and visiting cards, while keeping his website, www.JimNeglia.com, up to date.

After spending years researching his ancestry and finally gaining the knowledge of past generations, Jim Neglia can now begin to understand his connection to the past. Neglia learned about his relatives and their dedication to music, their passion in life, and in this book highlights two of his ancestors and their illustrious careers.

Are our abilities passed down from generation to generation, or are a family's talents developed during their formative years? The author takes the reader on a journey through eight generations of musicians to help answer that question. Among other things, Neglia explains how strong family genes are coupled with the nurturing of our talents by our elders.

Along with discussions on his ancestry and beliefs are journal entries and recountings of current events, including the crippling COVID-19 pandemic and its impact on the music industry. In the process, Neglia relays an amazing tale, weaving the past and the present to tell a story 200 years in the making, sharing his views on the complexities of his family's personalities by sharing intimate stories of life as a Neglia.

CPSIA information can be obtained
at www.ICGtesting.com
Printed in the USA
BVHW031053250222
630078BV00001B/15